"I am honored to endorse this book for my friend Holley Gerth. Not only is she a fabulous, relatable writer, but she is a gift to everyone who has had the opportunity to share a corner of life with her. . . . In *You're Already Amazing*, Holley invites you to settle in with her, to hear the words of Christ, and to walk away changed. I have a feeling you'll be calling her your friend by the time you finish the first chapter, and I also have the sense that you'll feel a peace in knowing what the Lover of your soul longs for you to embrace as reality. He created you just as you are, for purposes that will bless and honor him. We can all use that reminder!"

Angie Smith, Women of Faith speaker and author of
I Will Carry You and *What Women Fear*

"Simply put, this is a book for every woman. Every woman who feels a crack line somewhere in her heart. Every woman who needs to find her way back to hope, Jesus, and everything she was made to be in Christ. Holley Gerth is a fresh voice for every woman—she echoes the voice of our Father."

Ann Voskamp, New York Times bestselling author of
One Thousand Gifts

"Stepping out to be who God's called us to be is a faith dare. We can't make this journey alone, and because of Holley's book, we don't have to. Holley's words strike that beautiful balance of trusted confidante, biblical counselor, and encouraging BFF. *You're Already Amazing* gives our hearts permission to be at home with who we are and to receive God's love down deep where we crave it most."

Bonnie Gray, www.FaithBarista.com

"Holley Gerth turns words like a poet. Warm and personal, You're Already Amazing is a biblical, practical handbook for every woman's heart. I would love to read this again with a small group of women or high school girls."

Emily P. Freeman, author of *Grace for the Good Girl*

"Reading this book is like sitting down for a conversation with Holley—and trust me, that's a real treat. You'll get all her attentive compassion and empowering wisdom. Best of all, you'll end up believing the truth of her God-given message: You are amazing!"

Heather Gemmen Wilson, bestselling author and international speaker

"Holley has an amazing way of speaking to and captivating the heart of a woman. This inspirational book is a must read for any woman needing a huge dose of encouragement and new perspective on how amazing she really is!"

Janet Daughtry, co-founder, Biblical Coaching Alliance

"*You're Already Amazing* offers women a dare they can't refuse. In Holley's gentle, loving way, she challenges us to dismiss the lie we think about ourselves—the one that insists we aren't enough. And then she offers us the tools we need in order to believe that we are already amazing. I found freedom in her words."

Kristen Welch, author of *Don't Make Me Come Up There!*
and founder of Mercy House ministry

"When you're wondering who you are and why you are, this book is like the good friend who takes you out to coffee to help figure it out. Holley Gerth understands all the expectations we heap on ourselves and shows us how to lay them down one by one in favor of the relationship God is inviting us into. This book and its message are the most wonderful, encouraging, and comforting relief."

Lisa-Jo Baker, social media manager for DaySpring
and community manager for www.incourage.me

"I so appreciated Holley Gerth's heart as I read *You're Already Amazing*—a work full of encouragement, joy, and extremely helpful prompts that helped me overcome obstacles in my own heart. This book is a perfect addition to the library of any woman who wants to see genuine life change and experience it with joy alongside."

Mary DeMuth, author of *Beautiful Battle*

You're Already
Amazing

You're Already Amazing

Amazing

*Embracing Who You Are,
Becoming All God Created You to Be*

Holley Gerth

Revell

a division of Baker Publishing Group
Grand Rapids, Michigan

Published by Revell
a division of Baker Publishing Group
P.O. Box 6287, Grand Rapids, MI 49516-6287
www.revellbooks.com

Printed in the United States of America

Library of Congress Cataloging-in-Publication Data
Gerth, Holley.
    You're already amazing : embracing who you are, becoming all God created you to be / Holley Gerth.
        p. cm.
    Includes bibliographical references.
    ISBN 978-0-8007-2060-5 (pbk.)
    1. Christian women—Religious life. 2. Self-acceptance in women—Religious aspects—Christianity. I. Title.
BV4527.G466 2012
248.8′43—dc23   2011042690

The internet addresses, email addresses, and phone numbers in this book are accurate at the time of publication. They are provided only as a resource; Baker Publishing Group does not endorse them or vouch for their content or permanence.

In keeping with biblical principles of creation stewardship, Baker Publishing Group advocates the responsible use of our natural resources. As a member of the Green Press Initiative, our company uses recycled paper when possible. The text paper of this book is composed in part of post-consumer waste.

17   18   19   20   14   13

green press INITIATIVE

For amazing you

and the God who made you that way

Contents

Introduction

The Dare

Pssst ... pull up a chair and I'll tell you a secret. You'd better lean in close for this one.

Ready?

You don't have to *do* more, *be* more, *have* more.

I'm sure there are security alarms going off somewhere. You should probably hide this book when your in-laws come over. And this could be the makings of a Sunday morning scandal.

But it's true.

It's the kind of true that will change your life, set you free, and make you wake up smiling for the first time in a long time. I know because that's what it did for me (and believe me, for this non–morning girl that's nothing short of miraculous). I've seen it happen to a lot of other women too. I've read it in their words through thousands of comments on my blog. I've seen it in their faces as they sit on the couch in my counseling office. I've heard it in a new kind of laughter over coffee with friends.

So watch out, sister. If you keep reading, you just might be next.

Even if we've never met, I know this about you: you're a daughter of God, a holy princess, a woman created with strengths you've yet to fully grasp and a story that's still being written by the divine

Author himself. And if you really take hold of who you are and what you're called to do, there will be no stopping you. That's because there's no stopping him *in you*—and he's got bigger plans for your life than you've even imagined.

Okay, you've been warned.

If you're feeling brave, I dare you to read on . . .

1

A **Heart-to-Heart** Talk

My friend sits across the table at lunch. She's lovely, wonderful, a bringer of joy to my heart. Yet today there's little light in her eyes. She talks of endless juggling—kids, work, church, marriage, sex, groceries, and God.

She whispers, "Sometimes I don't even like my life. And I feel so guilty because I'm so blessed."

She speaks of reading books, doing studies, and listening to sermons that say she needs to give more, have more quiet time, find more friends.

"I try," she says. "I try so hard and I just fall further behind."

She describes her spirituality as a treadmill that keeps having the speed turned up. She runs faster and faster, only to become more exhausted.

As she shares, I think not of where she is going but of the One who is pursuing her heart. He stands just behind her, but she can hardly hear his voice above the whir of the track.

"Dear daughter," he whispers. "Come to me. You are weary and burdened. I will give you rest. You're already pleasing to me."

I tell her this and she pauses, sighs, leans into that truth for a moment. I watch the treadmill slow and then stop as she rests instead in the arms of grace.

A woman settles onto the couch in my counseling office. I can tell she's got something hard to say this week. She shifts back and forth. I see the words rolling around in her mind and finally making their way to her lips. She tells of abuse from those who should have protected her. Rejection instead of love. Names called in the privacy of her home and the public of the playground. Sticks and stones could break her bones, but it's words that have broken her heart. She finally comes up for air, and as the tears run a river down her cheeks, it seems a single lie follows their tracks.

"You could never be enough."

If it were audible it would be said with a hiss—the same one that has haunted Eve's daughters since the Garden. And within me I feel the response rising from a more Tender Voice.

"Tell her the truth."

So I do, and the rivers of tears become torrents, buckets of loss and fear poured out in that office. Empty and full, she looks up and smiles.

It's the first time I've ever seen her do so.

She writes me an email from across the world. I've never seen her face or even visited her continent. But we are more alike than different.

She tells me of feeling meaningless and wondering if she has anything at all to offer. She types, "Everyone else matters but me. Everyone else has something to offer but me. God must be so disappointed."

As I read her words I feel a physical ache in my chest, a longing for her to see what I can see in just a few sentences—that she has kindness, creativity, gifts, and strengths. She is brave, compassionate, and valuable.

I think of God placing his hand over hers as she types those sentences, wanting with all of his heart to replace those wounding words with new ones that reflect his love for her.

I type back, "Yes, you matter. No one can take your place. God made just one *you*, and this world needs you just as you are."

I hit "Send" and pray the truth will make its way straight to her heart.

Wherever I connect with women, it seems the same hurt is there. I recognize it well because I've felt it too.

I know what it's like to stare at the ceiling in the middle of the night and ask hard questions with few answers. I know what it's like to hide in the corner of the room, hoping no one will notice me, wondering if I'll ever be wanted. I know what it's like to wrestle with insecurity, guilt, and impossible standards of my own making. *I know.*

Yet there also came a point when my heart began knowing something deeper as well. In my desperation, I started asking God what he really wanted for his daughters. I searched the Scriptures, talked to women, pondered and prayed. I'm still trying to understand all of it and, quite clumsily, to fully live it. But what I discovered just may be the best news you'll ever hear.

So let's talk.

Would You Like to Have Coffee?

Imagine I ask you to have coffee with me—which is exactly what I do with my dearest friends. There's just something about sitting across a table from someone you truly care about that really gets a conversation going. (And if you're not a coffee drinker, then tea or a yummy dessert are perfectly acceptable substitutes.)

I call, text, or email: "Can we get together? There's something I'd really like to tell you."

We pick your favorite spot. I meet you at the door. We settle into a quiet corner. Order our favorite drinks. Swap small talk over mochas or tea.

Sip by sip we go deeper, until we land at the level of the heart...that place where it's hard to go in the middle of the busy and the broken.

I clear my throat, lean back, look you in the eyes, and say:

~ *"It's time you knew you're amazing."* ~

You smile, laugh awkwardly, glance at the ceiling. "I know, I know," you reply. "So kind of you to say."

I respond, looking at you more intently.

"I mean it's time you *really* knew. And there's more:

○ You're not only amazing.
○ You're enough.
○ You're beautiful.
○ You're wanted.
○ You're chosen.
○ You're called.
○ You've got what it takes ... not just to survive but to change the world."

By this time your fingers are wrapped around your cup. You stare down at the bottom of it, focused on the emptiness, wondering why these words are so hard to hear.

Finally, you ask, "Who told you that?"

And I respond, "The only One who really knows—Someone who loves you."

You're God's "Is Girl"

There's a pause in our conversation, and you point to a frame on the wall. It's a portrait of a woman taken by a professional photographer. The image makes it clear that she's the kind of girl who makes heads turn and smiles appear out of thin air. She looks entirely serene and effortlessly chic. We speculate that even grande mochas don't go to her hips.

"Okay," you laugh, "I could understand if you told her she's amazing. But me? I've got a lot of work to do. I'm not exactly the 'it girl.'"

"Good thing you're not," I casually respond.

You're a bit surprised. "What did you just say?"

"I said it's a good thing you're not the 'it girl.'" And with a twinkle in my eye, I lean in to tell you why.

Our culture is obsessed with the "it girl." She's defined as a woman who has it all together—whatever "it" is at the moment. We want to be like her and do what she does. We can't imagine anyone feeling the same way about us. Life becomes a competition to see who can be the prettiest, trendiest, and most stylish. In the corporate world, it's who can climb highest, fastest, farthest. In the church (don't think we're exempt) it's who can be the sweetest, godliest, most servant-hearted. Depending on the day or year, who that woman is changes. It's an endless game of "tag—you're it" that exhausts us all and makes us competitors rather than sisters.

But when we look at the kingdom of God, it's a different story. There aren't "it girls" (or guys). There are only "*is* girls." God looks at you and says, "She *is* loved, accepted, and valued. She *is* created just the way I wanted her to be."

Our biblical buddy Paul wrote letters to some of the first churches. He told early Christians that we're a body. Someone is a hand. Another person is a foot. There's no competition—only complementing and completion. Part of the beauty of that is how different we are from each other. As my friend Jennifer Leep says, "God creates each of us to be uniquely who we are—just like each part of the body is unique. We don't need more than one of a given body part. Nor would we want more than one. Sure, we have two hands and two feet. But not two *right* hands or two *left* feet. Each part of the body has a purpose that only it can fulfill. The same is true for us. That's a truth that's easy to understand *and easy to forget*."

Most People Don't

In my life, forgetting the truth we just talked about often starts with one phrase: "Most people don't . . ."

Those three words *ping, ping* in my mind over and over like pebbles against a glass window. When they do, I pause and consider, "It's true. Most people don't spend so much time sitting in front of a laptop and writing." And then it comes: "What's the matter with you? Why can't you relax and be more like most people?"

You've had these words thrown like stones at you too, haven't you?

Most people don't . . . wear themselves out in the kitchen because they believe a meal feeds hearts and fills bellies.

Most people don't . . . throw off their entire schedule because they take time to listen to the stranger in the grocery store who's having a hard day.

Most people don't . . . pore over spreadsheets until their eyes are red because they see numbers as a sort of art and a way of bringing order to a chaotic world.

It's true. Most people don't do what you do, love what you love, feel the kind of passion you feel about that thing.

I started thinking about this recently, and I realized we're in pretty good company if we feel like we're not like most people. After all:

- Most people don't . . . build an ark.
- Most people don't . . . lead people through the desert to the Promised Land.
- Most people don't . . . die on a cross to save the world.

But aren't we glad one person did each of these things?

If most people don't do what you do, and you're passionately pursuing Jesus with your life, then it's probably not just a human plan. The heartbeat of God is probably somewhere within it. We need you, just you, to fulfill that purpose, complete that project, bring that gift to the world in a way no one else can.

Most people don't . . . but you do.

In your own wonderful way, you're God's "is girl."

And that's amazing.

Putting the Pieces Together

Back at our corner table, a waitress stops by and asks if we need anything else. She lifts an empty cup from the table, revealing more of the surface beneath. It's a mosaic, hundreds of broken pieces placed together again to make a vibrant pattern.

I run my hand over the roughness and reflect, "This has been the hardest part for me."

You tilt your head and pull your brows together, a look of concern crossing your face. "What do you mean?"

"The brokenness in my life has sometimes made it difficult for me to believe I could ever be amazing."

I can relate to those scattered pieces on the tabletop because my life is made of much the same. Bits of hurt tossed here and there, dreams shattered. This has especially been true in the last five years or so. My husband and I have struggled with infertility all that time (and we still do). That kind of brokenness isn't a loss you mourn once and move on from; it stays.

As I drove home from work one day, the pain I felt seemed especially pointless, and in turn, my life did too. "God," I whispered, "how can you use me when I'm so broken?"

A song came on the radio that repeated a verse from Isaiah over and over again:

> *He was pierced for our transgressions,*
> *he was crushed for our iniquities;*
> *the punishment that brought us peace was on him,*
> *and by his wounds we are healed. (Isa. 53:5)*

I started singing along with the words. As I did it seemed God whispered to my soul, "You think you have to take what's broken and make it perfect in order to be used by me. But I think in a completely different way. I took what was perfect, my Son, and made him broken so that you could be whole. And because you belong to him, your brokenness can bring healing to others too."

I touch the mosaic again. "It's a crazy, upside-down way of thinking. But it's true. God has used my brokenness in ways I never expected. It's become part of who I am, a surprisingly beautiful part."

My friend and fellow writer Angie Smith can also relate to broken pieces. She shared a story on her blog *Bring the Rain* about smashing a pitcher and then piecing it back together again after the loss of her daughter:

> I began to realize that this pitcher was my life, and every piece was part of a story that God had chosen to put together. I started crying, and remembering things I thought I had forgotten. It took a long time to finish, but it was time well spent. Every nook and cranny whispered to me, until at last it stood in all its imperfection.
>
> *Here you are, Angie.*
>
> *You are mended. You are filled with my Spirit, and I am asking you to pour yourself out.*
>
> The image of my life as a broken pitcher was beautiful to me, but at the same time, it was hard to look at all of the cracks.
>
> I ran my fingers along them and told him I wish it had been different. How I wished I had always loved him, always obeyed him, always sought him the way I should. I was mad at the imperfections, years wasted, gaping holes where it should be smooth.
>
> But God, my ever-gracious God, was gentle and yet convicting as he explained.
>
> *My dearest Angie. How do you think the world has seen me? If it wasn't for the cracks, I couldn't seep out the way I do. I chose the pitcher. I chose you, just as you are.*[1]

God has put my heart together again too. It's not the same as before—but it's good. He's filled those empty spaces with his grace and, surprisingly, joy. Oh, sure, there are still days when I try to tear the table apart again and make it into something else I think I'd like better. But those days are fewer and farther in between.

I touch the seams between the pieces in the table again and say, "It's a good thing God can put us back together again. I'm totally craft challenged. I'm not even allowed to use a hot glue gun!"

We both laugh and then sigh, lost in our thoughts, wondering at the way God works. He doesn't just restore; he transforms. Beauty from ashes—or brokenness.

The End (and the Beginning)

By this time the coffee shop is almost empty. We take one last sip and make plans to get together again soon.

"Remember," I say as we walk toward the door, "it's true—you're already amazing."

You laugh, "Okay, I'll try to believe it. But you might need to say it a few more times."

"I will. I promise."

We step into early evening. The lights outside are just starting to really shine.

And maybe, just maybe, the ones inside are too.

2

Who Am I, *Really?*

Who am I?

It's a question we ask throughout our lives. Oh, maybe we don't use those exact words. But we're looking for the answer from the time we awkwardly enter the middle school cafeteria and hope for a table where we belong. It can drive us to fix our hair a certain way, date that boy, break that rule, join that club, or pursue that degree, and it can ultimately take us to the life we have now. Even as grown women, we still ask it. We just trade the junior high cafeteria for a women's retreat, corporate boardroom, or playgroup. No matter how many years go by, we still ask, "Who am I, *really?*"

And until we can answer that question, it's impossible to believe we're amazing.

I believe the desire to know who we really are has been placed within us by the heart of heaven itself. God wants us to understand who he created us to be so that we can fulfill the purpose he has for our lives. Sometimes we feel guilty for wishing we knew more about ourselves. After all, we're not supposed to focus on ourselves, right? I often hear women say, "That's selfish." But it's not the question that matters—it's what we do with the answer.

If you want to understand yourself just so that you can do whatever you'd like for your personal gain, then it's self-centered. If your intent is to love God, others, and yourself more, then knowing who you are is one of the most unselfish things you can do. And I have a feeling that second option is why you're reading this book. Yes? So push that guilt aside and give yourself permission to explore who God made you to be.

Once we decide we want to know who we are, we still wonder, "But how can I know who I am?" This chapter is designed to give you tools to help answer that question. The following pages are broken into sections that will give you an overview of three different parts of who you are: your strengths, your skills, and your "who." Each section includes an interactive tool that will help you apply what you've read specifically to you.

A little disclaimer: All the chapters in this book have interactive tools and exercises, and you have full freedom to use them in whatever way works best for you—whether that's doing them as you go, waiting until the end, or even (gasp!) skipping them completely. For a printable version of the tools and exercises, go to www.holleygerth.com/books. And if you're interested in going deeper, check out the guide in the back of the book. You can use it on your own, with a few friends, or in a group.

Your Strengths

When new clients come to me for counseling, I ask them to fill out a form. In one place it asks, "What is one of your strengths?" There are far more personal questions on the page, but that's the one that's most often left blank. Women walk through the door and apologize,

"I couldn't think of anything to put for that question." Whatever else we may talk about in our sessions, we always work on finding strengths. It's like mining for diamonds. I know those strengths are in there—we've just got to find them and bring them into the light.

It's the same way with you. Like I said before, I wish we could have coffee together so that I could find those strengths with you in person. You've got them. I know it. God does too. After all, he's the One who placed them within you.

So what exactly is a strength? *A strength is a personal characteristic that can be used on behalf of God in service to others.* Usually strengths are present throughout our lives but can be enhanced through experience or training. Strengths are part of *who we are* while skills are more about *what we do.*

· · · · · · · · · · *Find Your Strengths: 5 Minutes* · · · · · · · · ·

Circle three strengths that apply to you.

○ Adventurous	○ Fair	○ Organized
○ Athletic	○ Flexible	○ Positive
○ Brave	○ Forgiving	○ Protective
○ Calm	○ Friendly	○ Reflective
○ Capable	○ Frugal	○ Reliable
○ Caring	○ Funny	○ Resilient
○ Cheerful	○ Gentle	○ Resourceful
○ Considerate	○ Gracious	○ Responsible
○ Courageous	○ Hardworking	○ Sensitive
○ Creative	○ Helpful	○ Servant-hearted
○ Dedicated	○ Honest	○ Spontaneous
○ Determined	○ Hospitable	○ Supportive
○ Devoted	○ Imaginative	○ Talented
○ Easygoing	○ Intelligent	○ Thoughtful
○ Efficient	○ Kind	○ Trustworthy
○ Encouraging	○ Loving	○ Warm
○ Energetic	○ Loyal	○ Wise
	○ Mature	○ *Add your own...*

If you're still wondering if the words you circled are strengths, then you can put them through the STRENGTH test:

Service	*Does it help me serve God and others?*
Time	*Has it been present throughout much of my life?*
Relationships	*Do others see this?*
Energy	*Do I feel energized when I'm living this way?*
Natural	*Does this come naturally to me most of the time? Or do I know God has intentionally developed this in me even though it doesn't?*
Glory	*Does God ultimately get the glory from it?*
Trials	*Even in hard times, does it usually come through somehow?*
Heart	*Does this really feel like a core part of who I am?*

The Source of Your Strengths

How did you get your strengths? God created you with them. You are "fearfully and wonderfully made" (Ps. 139:14). Then he allows life experiences to develop your strengths even more.

For example, I love words. *Always have.* I don't like numbers. *Never have.* Are you nodding your head with me? Shaking it back and forth in disagreement? Marcus Buckingham and Donald O. Clifton, authors of *Now, Discover Your Strengths*, say there's a reason for your particular response. They explain that our brains are actually wired to approach life in certain ways: "By the age of three each of your hundred billion neurons have formed fifteen thousand synaptic connections with other neurons. . . . Your pattern of threads, extensive, intricate and unique, is woven."[1]

Pretty amazing, huh? Marcus and Donald go on to say that by age sixteen, half of these connections are lost. "Oh, no!" I thought when I first read that. But it's actually a great big, "Oh, yes!" to who God created you to be. The connections dropped allow you to focus intensely on the remaining ones, your strengths. As Marcus and Donald say,

> Your smartness and your effectiveness depend on how well you capitalize on your strongest connections. Nature forces you to shut down billions of connections precisely so that you can be freed up to exploit the ones remaining. Losing connections isn't something to be concerned about. Losing connections is the point.[2]

In essence, the most vibrant connections become our strengths, and those that fade away become our weaknesses. I love this because there are parts of me I wish I could change. (I'm sure no one else feels that way.) I don't have many decorating, details, or dinner-making connections in my brain. No, ma'am!

But it turns out that God has physically wired me with strengths that let me fulfill his purpose for my life. And he helps me do so by strategically creating certain weaknesses too. It gives "power made perfect in weakness" (see 2 Cor. 12:9) a whole new meaning. *Our divinely created strengths (fueled by God's power) are actually supported by our weaknesses, because if we were good at everything, we wouldn't focus on much of anything.*

Sigh of relief. Maybe no one else struggles with this, but it was some of the best news I've heard in a long time. For my husband's sake, I'm still going to try to keep those weaknesses a little in check. (Who made coffee without a filter last week because she's not so good at details? *Ahem.*) But I'm also going to celebrate who I am and who you are—fearfully and wonderfully made, strengths and weaknesses woven together just right.

Living in Your Strengths

Once we know our strengths, we can begin to feel a lot of pressure to maintain a certain standard. We tell ourselves, "I have to *always* be friendly." Or "I should *never* miss an opportunity to be kind." Then when we miss the mark, we're quick to condemn ourselves. But even in our areas of strength, we'll mess up. We'll fall short. We'll make mistakes. That's why there's grace.

And we don't have to muster up the power to live in our strengths ourselves. Philippians 4:13 says, "I can do all things through Christ who strengthens me" (NKJV). Jesus is the source of our strengths, and he's also the One who enables us to live in them each day. We don't have to force ourselves to be "on" all the time. Instead our focus can be on remaining "in" Christ. Just ask him to use your strengths to glorify him and serve others. And if you mess up, ask forgiveness and keep on going.

Also, be gentle with yourself. When we're tired, hungry, lonely, or afraid, our strengths can quickly flip to the other extreme. Passion becomes irritability. Sensitivity turns into worry. If you find yourself having a reaction that's not helpful, just stop and take a deep breath. Think about what you're feeling and what you need.

Rather than wishing you were different, stop and say, "I'm getting away from my strengths right now." Then ask yourself, "What do I need to do to change this reaction and respond out of one of my strengths instead?" Ask God for help, and then take action. *When you attack yourself, you side with the enemy.* God is always for you—that means you can be too. We'll all slip out of our strengths at times. The key is just getting back into them as quickly as possible. Receiving God's grace and giving it to ourselves speeds up that process.

The goal is not perfection. It's simply to be in an intimate relationship with Christ each day, fully embrace who he created us to be, and seek to fulfill the purpose he has for us. He is our greatest strength—and the One who enables us to live out all the other strengths he's placed within us.

> *Hey, you . . .*
> *The one wondering if you've got strengths.*
> *You do.*
> *The one questioning if God really even wants to use you.*
> *He does.*
> *You've got gifts to offer the world.*
> *Things that are good and right and true.*
> *No one else can make a difference like you can.*
> *Like you already are.*
> *Dare to believe it.*
> *Dare to receive it.*
> *Stand tall, be strong, just go out there and be you*
> *in your own wonderful way.*
> *Today.*

Your Skills

Now that you know your strengths, what do you do with them? Chances are, you're already doing something. Strengths are made to be expressed. We call those expressions *skills*. *A skill is a strength expressed in a specific way that builds up others and benefits the kingdom.*

Skills can get overlooked. Besides being made fun of in the movie *Napoleon Dynamite* (okay, that was pretty hilarious), they can sometimes seem less than spiritual.

For example, you might wonder, "How does something like cooking help the kingdom?" (Besides potlucks, which are just about the best kind of goodness this side of heaven.) In the DaySpring Cards creative area where I worked, this verse stayed on the wall for many years:

> I have filled him with the Spirit of God, with skill, ability
> and knowledge in all kinds of crafts. (Exod. 31:3 NIV 1984)

This verse reveals that God's hand is in our skills, in the ordinary things we do. *And they matter.* A lot. We don't all have the same skills. For example, the "all kinds of crafts" part doesn't quite fit me. If the word *craft* appears in my life, it starts with a "K" and ends with me making macaroni and cheese.

To help us figure out our skills, I've got another list. Take a look and find yours.

· · · · · · · · · · **Find Your Skills: 5 Minutes** · · · · · · · · · ·

Circle three skills that apply to you.

○ Acting	○ Decorating	○ Persevering
○ Adapting	○ Empathizing	○ Persuading
○ Administering	○ Encouraging	○ Planning
○ Advising	○ Evaluating	○ Prioritizing
○ Analyzing	○ Expressing	○ Problem-solving
○ Appreciating	○ Growing	○ Protecting
○ Assembling	○ Guiding	○ Relating
○ Believing	○ Helping	○ Responding
○ Building	○ Imagining	○ Risk taking
○ Challenging	○ Influencing	○ Serving
○ Cleaning	○ Initiating	○ Sharing
○ Collaborating	○ Leading	○ Speaking
○ Cooking	○ Listening	○ Supporting
○ Communicating	○ Maintaining	○ Teaching
○ Connecting	○ Managing	○ Training
○ Constructing	○ Motivating	○ Writing
○ Coordinating	○ Negotiating	○ *Add your own . . .*
○ Counseling	○ Nurturing	
○ Creating	○ Organizing	

Connecting Strengths and Skills

Skills Circles can be a fun way to connect strengths with skills. Draw a circle and write one of your strengths in the middle. Then draw small circles around the edge and write related skills in them. Here's a personal example:

The size of each circle is related to how much I express that strength through the skill. For example, I write a lot more than I speak.

Have fun with this! Doodle, put these in your journal, write them on napkins next time you're stuck on a plane. This isn't meant to be a big project—just a little tool.

We usually express the same core strength in many different ways. That reveals a lot about who we are and what God has called us to do in our lives.

Watch out, world! We've got skills and we're not afraid to use them. (Except for the hot glue gun. I'm still not going there. You fabulously talented crafty people handle that one for me, okay?)

Skills for Different Seasons

A few years ago I had the opportunity to help women go through a study called The Significant Woman: Pursuing God and His Unique Design for Your Life. During the study, many of the women confided things like, "I know one of my strengths is being creative. But right now I don't even have time to take a shower because I have a new baby! I feel guilty for not doing what God wants me to do."

While strengths stay consistent throughout our lives, the skills that display them vary depending on the season we're in and the specific assignment God has given us. For example, when I asked those women questions, I found that they were still being creative! They told stories to their toddlers as they tucked them in, came up with new games to play, or just found interesting solutions to the everyday issues that come with having little ones. That strength was still coming through loud and clear—it just looked different than before, so it was harder for them to recognize. If you're in a season of life where you're not getting to use a particular skill, ask yourself, "What is the strength behind this skill?" Then see if there's another way you're already expressing this strength or one you'd like to try.

While what we do may change, the reason we do it stays the same. "Whatever you do, do it all for the glory of God" (1 Cor. 10:31). King David had the skill of shepherding. He did that first with sheep and then as a ruler of God's people. Peter had the skill of fishing—first with actual fish and then with hearts. God will use you in a lot of different ways throughout your life.

Here's a little confession: I can tend to focus too much on my skills, especially in the busy times of my life. I spin my wheels, wear myself out, and try to do everything at once. When I finally slow down enough to hear God's voice, it seems what he often whispers to my heart is, *"Holley, I want your heart more than your hands."*

Yes, our skills matter. Yes, they are important to God's purpose for our lives. But in the end, what he wants most is simply *us*. Our hearts. Our dreams. Our days. Then what we do with our skills is just a natural response—and ordinary activities such as cooking or cleaning become just as sacred as leading a church or going on a mission trip.

*I've been thinking of you right there in the middle of
    the ordinary . . .
changing diapers, writing reports,
driving, cleaning, fixing, blessing.
Ordinary is hard for me.
Is it ever hard for you?
I like the new.
The exciting.
And yet it seems God has been whispering
that I need to look at the ordinary with new eyes.
All that seems small can be really BIG.
And what we do every day
matters more than we know,
more than we see.
You are making a difference.
You deserve to be applauded—
for just digging in, doing what you do,
keeping at it no matter what.
So from the bottom of my heart . . .
THANK YOU
for all you do.
(I've got a feeling it brings joy to God too.)*

Your "Who"

Our strengths and skills aren't meant just for us. So the next step is to take some time to consider who shares our lives and stories. Before we do so, I'd like to bust the myth among women that goes something like this: "Everyone else has lots of relationships, but not me."

Facebook, Twitter, and all the other social media sites out there can make it seem as if the whole world is one big party and we're not invited. The enemy can use that to lie to us and make us feel alone. But it's not true.

According to an article in *USA Today*, 25 percent of Americans do not have even one friend they can confide in. Including family, the average number of close relationships is still only two.[3] What I want to highlight here is this: *you are doing okay in your relationships.*

That being said, let's take a closer look at the relationships in your life. I've created a little diagram to help us out.

Your Social Circles: 5 Minutes

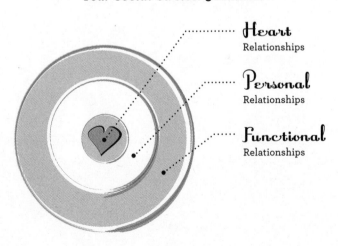

Heart
Relationships

Personal
Relationships

Functional
Relationships

○ **Heart Relationships**

This is your inner circle, those with whom you can truly share who you are, the ups and downs. Some family members and your close friends would be here.

○ **Personal Relationships**

These people share your life in your neighborhood, church, work, family, and so on. You care about each other, but they are more casual relationships than the first group.

○ **Functional Relationships**

These connections are very casual, and interactions have a practical purpose. You might call them acquaintances.

Think about names that would be in each of the circles above and write them there if you'd like. You don't have to include everyone you know—just enough to give you a broad overview of who's in your life and how you're connecting to others.

When we look at the life of Jesus, we see he had different types of relationships just like those in the previous chart. He had three disciples who were closest to him, then the twelve, the forty, and the multitudes.

Like our skills, our relationships will vary with the seasons and stages of our lives. When my husband and I first got married, we moved to a new town. I'd had several close friends in college but now suddenly found myself alone. It took several years of trying to connect with people (and a lot of praying!) before I formed new bonds where I now lived. So if you find yourself in a season of fewer relationships, give yourself grace and know it's most likely not about you. If you find you're intentionally holding back or avoiding people, talk to a counselor or someone you trust so your heart can heal and you can reach out again.

Connections to others impact our lives now and our legacies forever. As DaySpring cofounder Dean Kerns once said, "All we take with us into eternity are our relationships with God and each other."

Who You're Called to Serve

After you know your strengths (who you are) and skills (what you do) as well as understanding the relationships in your life, then you're ready to explore who you're specifically called to serve.

Yes, we're all called to love each other. And yet there's usually a group of people that has a special place in your heart. You might love working with kids, women, older adults, or inner-city youth. Knowing your *who* can help you make strategic choices about which opportunities to pursue and which to pass up.

Lisa-Jo Baker (who blogs at www.thegypsymama.com) is an amazing woman who has found her *who*. Raised in South Africa, she's done humanitarian work all over the world. Right in the middle of that journey, she discovered that she felt deeply called to serve moms with young kids. She sent me this email:

> I am at an incredible leadership conference in the Pacific Northwest. There are primarily men here, and they are discussing some groundbreaking work their organizations have done to bring justice to the poor and afflicted. For many years that is the kind of work I have been involved in also.
>
> But I have consistently felt this call on my heart to speak into the lives of women. Young mothers and wives who feel that what they do isn't important. So I blog. I write my heart out to this beautiful audience who need to be encouraged as I wish someone had done for me. Because young mothers and struggling women have great needs too. And it is my delight to be used by God to be part of the plan for meeting them.[4]

A few months after writing this email, Lisa-Jo became the social media manager for www.incourage.me, a website for the hearts of women. One of the other cofounders and I had been praying about who would be the right person to step into that role. In one of those rare moments, it seemed God almost audibly put Lisa-Jo's name on my heart. Without knowing anything, Lisa-Jo sent me another email saying she was resigning from her current position and asking us to keep her in mind if anything ever became available with (in)courage. When we called Lisa-Jo and shared that we had already been thinking of her, the "yes!" she responded with came easily because she knew (in)courage reached the exact group of people she felt called to serve.

While it seemed to happen quickly, Lisa-Jo found her *who* through a journey that took years. The same is often true of us. And yet there are usually glimpses along the way. Our heart is drawn to a particular group. We get excited when we know we'll be around a certain type of people. We feel at home with kids and out of place with teens. We love serving seniors but would rather skip out on nursery duty. We feel drawn to families rather than individual women. There are clues that lead us to who God wants us to serve.

· · · · · · · · · · · **Find Your Who: 5 Minutes** · · · · · · · · · · ·

- I feel especially drawn to:

- I'm at my best when I'm with:

- God has given me a tender spot in my heart for:

- My strengths and skills seem to help:

What you wrote might be very general (for example, "my family" or "women"), or it might be very specific ("children with special needs under the age of five"). Either way is okay.

Also, your *who* may change throughout your life. Right now you might be focused on toddlers because you've got three of them! Later on, you might shift your focus to mentoring college students.

It's also okay if you don't find a specific *who* right now. As mentioned before, we're all called to love each other. So if nothing comes to mind here, just serve whoever is in your life right now!

When an opportunity that seems to fit with your strengths, skills, and *who* comes along, you can use the tools in this chapter as filters to see if it's really in the center of what you're created to do. If it is, you can be fairly sure God is giving you the green light! If not, ask him if he specifically wants you to accept it as a special assignment that's outside of what you're called to do most of the time.

> your strengths **+** your skills **+** who you're called to serve
> **=** you making a difference in the world in your own
> amazing way

God's Heart for Who You Really Are

Even when we know our strengths, skills, and how we best connect with others, it can still be intimidating to think about living all of that out. That's especially true if we're a bit on the insecure side (I am).

Here comes a confession: *I'm intimidated by you.* And by you, I mean women. Put me in a room of my peers, and it won't be long before my hands are sweaty and I'm shaking in my boots (yes, the cute ones I bought from TJ Maxx in the hopes they'd somehow hypnotize everyone into liking me—you know what I'm talking about).

It got so bad I even took drastic measures a few summers ago. Disclaimer: There is some serious dorkiness coming in the next few sentences. If you're offended by that, you should stop reading now.

I went to the library and checked out all the social skills books. The ones like *How to Have Friends and Influence People without Relying on Your TJ Maxx Boots*. And I read *all* of them. I know—don't say I didn't warn you.

Through my ambitious pursuit of coolness, I discovered that my insecurities came from a much deeper place than an inability to make coherent small talk at times. What I thought might be some sort of social ailment turned out to be a spiritual one.

Inside a voice whispered, "You're not enough." Depending on the day, an extra word might be thrown into that sentence:

○ You're not *pretty* enough.
○ You're not *outgoing* enough.
○ You're not *likeable* enough.

So I kept spinning my wheels on an endless treadmill. I'd make progress in one area, only to realize I had miles to go in another. Exhausted, I finally began pondering and praying.

"Lord," I asked, "why do women feel as if we're not enough?"

It seemed I heard a whisper in response: *"Because they're not."*

For a moment I thought I had some holy static happening.

"Excuse me, God, it sounded like you said we're not enough. Could you repeat that, pretty please?"

Again, gently and firmly, "You are not enough."

By then I started thinking perhaps my heart had dialed the wrong number and the devil was on the line. But in that pause it seemed God finished the sentence: "You are not enough . . . *in me you are so much more.*"

○ We are *much more* than pretty . . . we are wonderfully made.
○ We are *much more* than likeable . . . we are deeply loved.
○ We are *much more* than okay . . . we are daughters of the King.

I think the enemy tricks us into believing we are not enough because he knows if we discover the truth, we'll be unstoppable.

If you've embraced that lie like I did, then together we can start trading it for the truth. We are chosen, cherished, created women who have all we need to fulfill God's plans for our lives. He has made us just as he wants us to be. We have something to offer that no one else can bring . . . and the world is waiting.

Girls, let's stop shaking in our boots and instead start standing tall for him together.

Let's use our strengths, skills, and relationships to make a difference.

Let's be who we are, *really*.

I can't do it alone—are you with me?

3

Why Is It So Hard to Believe I'm Amazing?

The scene is set. God has created the world in seven glorious days. Adam and Eve live in Paradise. And then the devil shows up with a single question: "Did God really say . . . ?" (Gen. 3:1). Insecurity makes its debut. Eve responds, then reconsiders. "The woman was convinced" (Gen. 3:6 NLT).

Everything changes forever.

I find it interesting that the enemy didn't blatantly tempt Eve. He didn't ask, "So, how about we head off to Las Vegas and run wild?" He was much more subtle. And his question is hauntingly familiar. I've heard other versions:

"Did God really say you have what it takes?"

"Did God really say you're loved?"

"Did God really say who you are is okay?"

And, like Eve, I often respond, reconsider, and become convinced. What if Eve had said, "Yep, God sure did say that, and I'm not listening to another word. Hit the road, buster"?

What if *we* said that?

"Yes, God really did say I can do all things through Christ" (see Phil. 4:13).

"Yes, God really did say he loves me with an everlasting love" (see Jer. 31:3).

"Yes, God really did say I am fearfully and wonderfully made" (see Ps. 139:14).

Everything could change forever.

I've never met a woman who found it easy to believe she's amazing. I'm not talking about the puffed-up pride we sometimes see from celebrities (that's really just another form of insecurity). I mean "I truly know who I am in Christ, embrace that fully, and live in it completely all the time." I used to think I had to find a silver bullet that would kill my insecurity and replace it with confidence. I now believe that because we're all Eve's daughters, this insecurity is something we'll face throughout our lives. Can we have victory? Yes, my sisters, we can. But it's not a one-time, easy fix. It's a battle. This chapter is all about equipping you to win again and again.

So first of all, let's drop that guilt that we struggle with this, okay? Even Jesus was tempted, and he was perfect. We're all going to wrestle with our identities, feel drawn to insecurity, and want to fill those holes within us in other ways. That's not a sin. What matters is what we do next. We have a choice between living in the truth or giving in to the flesh. And what we pick ultimately shapes us and the course of our lives.

Can we pause for a little confession here? I have been putting off this chapter. Yes, ma'am. I've had one of *those* weeks. You know, the kind that makes you want to polish off gallons of ice cream at a time, hide under the covers, and/or run off to a desert island (as long as it has plenty of ice cream too)?

Oh, yeah. I'm there. And I have felt anything *but* amazing. Yet God keeps tapping me on the shoulder and reminding me that what I write is just as much for my healing as it is for yours. I'm on this journey with you. He put some things on my heart that helped me, and I believe they'll help your heart too. Let's walk this road of words together, friend, and see where he wants to take us. Feel free to bring a spoon and some hot fudge with you if it helps.

Beyond Eve: Uncovering the Other Lies in Our Lives

From the moment we take our first breath as a beautiful baby girl, the enemy wants to suffocate our souls with the question, "Did God really say . . . ?" As our lives unfold, all of us experience the lies that come from that question in many different ways.

When you're a child, you accept everything you hear as true. Santa Claus? Of course! Easter Bunny? Yes! A fairy that leaves money under your pillow when you lose a tooth? Let's stay awake and try to see her! Over time those beliefs change because someone, whether a kid on a playground or a loving parent, tells us the truth. But there are many other lies we believe as children that don't ever get replaced.

You're not good enough.

You'll never amount to anything.

You don't fit in here . . . or anywhere.

Those lies are just as much a myth as Santa Claus and the Easter Bunny. But many of us never have anyone take us aside and say, "Hey, that's not true. This is what's real."

We all have lies we carry around inside us. Usually they're so familiar we don't even pay much attention to them. Pause for a moment and ask God to show you some of the lies you've believed about yourself. You can even write one below.

○ A lie my heart sometimes still hears is:

_____

_____

Whoever said "sticks and stones may break my bones, but words will never hurt me" must not have experienced childhood. Sentences slung at our souls wound deeply. I imagine you felt a sting as you filled in the blank above.

Some of my lies? *"You're so ugly." "No one likes you."* Ouch. As I revisited those lies recently, I pictured God, with his hand over my heart, touching the places where those syllables still sting. And a passage from the Gospels came to mind (see John 8:1–11). A woman accused is brought to Jesus. The leaders are ready to stone her. But Jesus "stooped down and wrote in the dust with his finger" (John 8:6 NLT). Jesus said whoever had never sinned should cast the first stone. *And they all walked away.*

What Christ wrote in the dust is a mystery. But whatever it was, *I know it was truth.* And now we stand as women accused. The enemy is ready to throw stones at us. In the dust of our hearts, I picture Jesus writing truth that covers those accusing words:

- Loved
- Accepted
- Chosen
- Mine

My eyes are overflowing a bit now (as I imagine those of the woman accused did too) with happy tears of freedom and grace. Others may speak into our lives. But Jesus has the final say. He covers the lies with love. May he heal us and help us to believe.

The accusations and lies in our lives come in different ways. Some are completely undeserved. For example, insensitive parents or insecure peers may tear us down to build themselves up. Other lies slip in through poor choices of our own and remain long after we've been forgiven.

Whatever the source, God's intent remains the same: to replace those lies with truth. While we can't cover every lie in this chapter, let's take a look at a few that women commonly struggle with and replace them with truth instead.

Lie #1: "I Have to Be Perfect"

I know Perfectionism. Let's call her "Ms. P" for short. She showed up in my life somewhere in the middle of elementary school and decided to stick around. Do you know her too? Oh, on the outside she's prim and proper. But beneath all that she's a bossy, inconsiderate, joy-stealing, lie-telling, impossible-to-please taskmaster who's never satisfied. She doesn't play well with others. I don't know why I kept her around for so long. I tried to get her to leave a few times, but she always came back—until I found some truth that finally sent her packing.

You see, Ms. P liked to quote a verse to me (no surprise there—the devil did it when he tried to tempt Jesus in the wilderness). Her favorite Scripture was, "Be perfect, therefore, as your heavenly Father is perfect" (Matt. 5:48). Every time I heard those words, I thought about how I was falling short and must try harder.

But I finally decided to look a little closer at what that verse might really mean. I looked for other verses that used the word *perfect*. Lo and behold, look what was hiding in Hebrews: "By one sacrifice he has made perfect forever those who are being made holy" (10:14). What? I've already been made perfect? I thought at first my Bible might have a typo. But it turns out it's true. I've already been made perfect. And so have you.

Here's how it works: There's only One who is perfect. To be perfect, I'd have to be him. But wait—"I no longer live, but Christ lives in me" (Gal. 2:20). When I gave my life to Jesus, he gave his to me too. In God's eyes, I'm as perfect as Christ. All that sin? It's settled once and for all. Whew. Jesus shows Ms. P to the door and says, "I'll take it from here."

Also, the Hebrew word for "perfect" is different than our typical Western definition. It actually speaks more to the concept of being "complete" and how we are all we need to be in Christ.

Does that mean we're off the hook and can do whatever we want? Nope, that's where the second part of the verse from Hebrews comes in. We've been made perfect—check—but we're still in the process of being made holy. God's goal in our lives is *growth*.

So what's the difference between growth and our typical idea of "perfection"?

- ° *Perfectionism is all or nothing.*
- ° Growth is little by little.
- ° *Perfectionism is all about the goal.*
- ° Growth is more about the journey.
- ° *Perfectionism is about outward appearances.*
- ° Growth is about what happens on the inside.
- ° *Perfectionism is about what we do.*
- ° Growth is about who we're becoming.

I love the verse in Proverbs that says, "The path of the righteous is like the morning sun, shining ever brighter till the full light of day" (4:18).

Growth in our lives often looks like this chart:

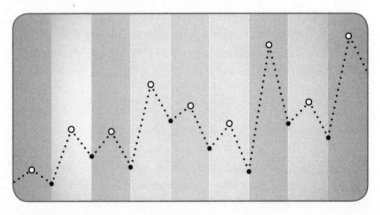

We go through peaks and valleys. We make some progress and then slip up. When that happens, *it feels like we're all the way back at the bottom*. But we're not—we're further along than we were before. We've gained new wisdom, developed our strengths a bit more, and leaned a little harder into God.

If Ms. P could draw on the previous chart, she'd make a red line across the top, and anything below it would be failure to her. But God sees our lives in a much different way. The red he places over our lives is the blood of his Son, and it covers us completely. Then he takes our hands, calls to our hearts, and says, "Let's go! I want to share life with you—just as you are, every step of the way."

Why You Don't Have to Be Perfect

I know Perfectionism.
She calls my name and says,
*   "You will never be good enough."*
And sometimes I listen.
I cower in a corner.
Or I endlessly run.
But it's always about fear.
Then these words stop me in my tracks,
grab me by the heart,
and invite grace to speak instead:
*   Perfect love casts out fear* (1 John 4:18)
I don't have to be perfect.
I only need to be perfectly loved.
And I am.
*   So are you*

Lie #2: "I Need to Be More Like Her"

Let's pretend we're sitting at a middle school lunch table, eavesdropping on giggly girls.

"My boyfriend is captain of the football team."

"I found the coolest jeans last weekend!"

"I got an A on the science test."

Is anyone else's heart racing just thinking about being back there? Good grief! Okay, I've regained my composure. The point is that as women we compare. A lot.

We tend to berate ourselves for this tendency. But really, I just think it's part of how we're wired.

Women were created by God to be inherently relational. This means we're always checking in, asking ourselves, "How's she doing? How's she doing? How's she doing?"

This is a reflection of our tender hearts and compassionate natures. It's a beautiful thing that makes us excellent mamas, wives, and friends. Where we get tripped up is when we follow that first question with, "How am I doing compared with her?"

Hold up. That's not helpful.

If we fall short, then we're insecure.

If we're doing better, then we're prideful.

If her life seems harder, then we don't feel entitled to our pain.

God's answer? Focus on him and his plan for your life.

There's a little scene at the end of the Gospel of John that I find a bit funny (it's okay to think that, right?). Jesus and Peter are having a heart-to-heart. Another disciple walks up, and in his typical style, Peter asks, "What about him, Lord?" Jesus has an even better question: "What is that to you?" And then, "As for you, follow me" (John 21:21–22 NLT).

Your story and strengths belong to you. God doesn't compare them (or you) to anyone else, and you don't have to either. Big sigh of relief. So as we explore our strengths together (and live them out with others), let's go for these three steps: share, care, prayer. And skip the compare. (Unless you get the coolest jeans on sale. Comparing prices totally doesn't count. You'd better reveal the deal, sister. I'm just saying.)

Lie #3: "I Don't Have Anything to Offer"

Y'all, I am terrible at holidays. Decorating makes me hyperventilate. My gift-selection skills are challenged. I can't sing worth a hoot. My one redeeming quality is that I can make some serious treats. Yes, ma'am. So a few years ago I got a truffle recipe from a friend. It involves a package of Oreos, cream cheese, and melted chocolate. Easy-peasy, I thought.

So I slaved away in the kitchen making my confections, imagining that I would soon get a phone call that went something like this: "What, Martha? Did you say you'd like to have me in the studio tomorrow? Well, I already booked with Rachael. Maybe next year." Needless to say, the phone did not ring, and it's a good thing, because when I got done . . . those were the ugliest truffles ever!

Horrified, I determined in my heart that I would sneak them onto the "free food" table at work and no one would be any wiser. Alone in my shame at my desk the next day, I heard an excited group of ladies talking outside of my area.

"I don't know who made them! We've been trying to find out all day!"

"Yes, they're amazing. I've just got to get the recipe for those truffles."

Say what?

It turns out my ugly truffles were a hit. I decided to out myself to the shock and delight of my co-workers. As I sat back down at my desk, it seemed God whispered, "This isn't just about the truffles."

I thought about how I do the same thing with other areas of my life. When parts of my heart or life don't measure up to my expectations, I tend to hide them. But what if someone would be blessed by what I have to share and they miss out because I hide it?

I'm thinking most of you are Holiday Queens who are far superior to me in making all the seasons of the year bright. But maybe, just maybe, you've got a little bit of the "ugly truffle complex" going on somewhere in your life too. By that I mean there's some part of you that God has said is "fearfully and wonderfully made" (Ps. 139:14), but you're just not quite sure about that yet. Women seem to be pretty good at agreeing with God unless he's talking nice about us. Can I get an "Amen"?

....

Let's put all we've got on the table for him and share it with our whole hearts. I may never be hot stuff when it comes to holidays, but with God's help I hope I can get a little better at living in the truth.

One of the biggest lies the enemy tries to tell us is that we don't have anything worthwhile to offer. Girls, we do. And God says it's good.

(I know you just kept reading in the hopes of getting that recipe. So let's all say thank you to my friend Jennifer Moore for giving it to me. Her truffles turn out lovely—but we won't hold that against her.)

· · · · · · · · · · · **Sweet & Simple Truffles** · · · · · · · · · ·

- ° 1 16-ounce package of Oreo cookies
- ° 1 8-ounce package cream cheese, softened
- ° 16 ounces semisweet baking chocolate, melted

Directions:

Completely crush Oreos and place in a bowl. Add cream cheese. Mix until blended. Roll cookie mixture into 1-inch balls. Dip in chocolate and place on wax paper to cool. Decorate truffles as desired.

Refrigerate until firm, about one hour. Eat them all, or keep refrigerated.

Lie #4: "Being Confident Will Make Me Prideful and Selfish"

It's the Last Supper. Jesus is headed to the cross. But first he washes his disciples' feet:

> Jesus knew that the Father had put all things under his power, and that he had come from God and was returning to God; so he got up from the meal, took off his outer clothing, and wrapped a towel around his waist. After that, he poured water into a basin and began to wash his disciples' feet. (John 13:3–5)

Did you catch that first line? Jesus was secure in who he was and whose he was, and that enabled him to freely serve. There's a myth that goes something like this: "Confidence will make you selfish." We fear becoming prideful, forgetting others, pursuing our own agendas. But here's the secret Jesus shows us: true confidence *leads to service.*

Insecurity does just what it sounds like—turns us inward. We focus on ourselves, our appearance, our house, our talents . . . you get the picture. I imagine you really want to do all you can to help, serve, and be humble. Me too. If so, then we need to be secure, confident, and assured that we're loved. Easy? Not at all. Life changing? Yes, ma'am. And you won't become prideful, I promise. I know, I've worried about that too.

Pride is really just another form of insecurity. It's an effort to puff ourselves up so we seem bigger (and therefore feel safer). *If we want to become more unselfish, we've got to believe what God says about us.* Because when we do, we'll be able to stop looking inward and instead focus upward and outward on him as well as others.

Is this scary to you? Good grief, I feel like I'm going to hyperventilate. But we'll be okay. We're just scared because we've never thought about things this way before; it's unfamiliar territory. And what's unknown is always scary. But as we practice this, lean into God's love, and ask him to show us a new way of living, that fear will go away. I promise. And what's even better, *God promises.* "For God did not give us a spirit of timidity, but a spirit of power, of love and of self-discipline" (2 Tim. 1:7 NIV 1984). That sounds a lot like true confidence to me.

I'm ready to take the risk of thinking about all of this differently. Will you try it with me?

Lie #5: "I Am Who Others Say I Am"

We tend to accept what others say about us as the truth about who we are. And it may be—as long as it aligns with what God says about us too.

Think back to those lies you thought about at the beginning of this chapter, the ones that still sting your soul when you think of them. Now picture Jesus saying them to you. "He would never say that!" you're probably thinking. And you're right. There is no condemnation in Christ, so if someone else has spoken condemning words over you, then they are not true—no matter how real they may feel.

We talked about how as children we believed whatever we were told. The apostle Paul describes it this way:

> When I was a child, I talked like a child, I thought like a child, I reasoned like a child. When I became a man, I put the ways of childhood behind me. For now we see only a reflection as in a mirror; then we shall see face to face. Now I know in part; then I shall know fully, even as I am fully known. (1 Cor. 13:11–12)

At some point, we have to deliberately choose to put those lies behind us. As Paul also says, until we're in heaven we won't see the complete picture—even about who we are. But we can begin to look into God's truth and ask him to show us what we need to know. This process takes time. It's not simple. It will feel awkward, uncomfortable, and as if what you're telling yourself isn't real at all. Your emotions will be the last to get on board.

God created our brains in amazing ways. When you think in certain ways, your mind makes literal, physical pathways. Think of it as building a road. As you grow up and new situations present themselves, your brain naturally goes the way of least resistance. It returns to those well-worn patterns. When you decide to replace lies with the truth, you're really creating new pathways in your brain. Think of it as constructing another road and letting grass grow over the original one. It takes time and perseverance. But it is possible. The hard work that it requires means holding on to the truth no matter what your emotions may try to tell you instead.

· · · · · · · · · · · *Replace the Lie: 5 Minutes* · · · · · · · · ·

○ A lie I've believed:

....

○ The truth God wants me to remember instead:

....

○ Scripture that shares this truth:

....

○ God has the ultimate word on who you are—not your spouse, friends, parents, co-workers, or spiritual leaders or even you. And he declares you're loved, valuable, accepted, and irreplaceable.

Did God really say . . . ?
Oh, yes, he did!

In Case You Ever Wonder

You question . . .
Is who I am okay?
>   *You're more than okay—you're His.* (Ps. 139:14)

You ask . . .
Do I have what it takes?
>   *You've got all you need.* (2 Pet. 1:3)

You wonder . . .
Can I do this?
>   *You can do all things.* (Phil. 4:13)

So go for it, girl.
Dare to make that difference,
take that step, follow that dream.
God will go with you—
>   *and love will see you through.*

Why Do I Feel This Way?

A woman walks into my counseling office. She talks of loss in her life. As tears slip down her cheeks, she grabs a tissue and says, "But I shouldn't feel this way."

Another woman arrives later in the day. She describes abuse and wrongs against her that have left deep scars on her heart. Her voice gets louder until she stops midsentence and says, "But I shouldn't feel this way."

A final client steps through the door and talks of a new opportunity. It's way out of her comfort zone. She starts to explore the unknown, then folds her shaking hands and says, "But I shouldn't feel this way."

I've responded like this too. Emotions knock on the door of my heart, and I turn them away. I hear old lines spoken by well-meaning people, like "If you're not smiling, you won't be a witness for Jesus" or "If you feel fear, you're not showing faith."

But in each of the scenarios above, the emotion was just a message about what that woman was experiencing.

For the first woman, sadness was saying, "You've experienced a loss."
For the second, anger was declaring, "You've been wronged."
And for the third, fear was cautioning, "You've got an exciting opportunity—but there are risks involved too."

Those emotions hopefully prompt the first woman to seek comfort, the second to tend to her wounds so she can eventually forgive, and the third to pray and plan as she moves ahead.

Of course, we also have positive emotions—joy at a wedding, contentment around the dinner table with those we love, enthusiasm as we begin a new job. Those uplifting feelings tell us important things too. *All* of our emotions are gifts from God to help us process *everything* we experience.

Emotions are also a big part of what makes you amazing. They allow you to respond to life in deeply personal ways. They connect you with others. They reflect your awesome Maker.

Research has shown that there are six universal emotions: anger, fear, disgust, amusement, sadness, and surprise.[1] How we display those emotions shows up in facial expressions that are recognizable in even the most remote parts of the world. The women I described above could walk through any door in any country and their feelings would be clear to those around them. Isn't that incredible? Our emotions display our hearts—our beautiful, broken, blessed, glorious hearts.

Your Approach to Emotions

Beyond the common emotional ground shared by all humanity, how we experience and express our feelings varies widely. Think of each basic emotion like a color. Give a box of crayons to a class of kindergarteners, and they'll all recognize red but use it in very different ways.

We approach emotions in a similar fashion. Some of us grab all the colors every chance we get, while others are more careful and methodical. Again, picture that kindergarten class. One little girl may be wildly scribbling a rainbow while another daintily fills in the details. Doesn't that image make you smile? It made me grin as I wrote it. There's something about recognizing our quirks and differences that brings us joy. I believe it does the same for God. After all, he's the One who created them.

So let's take a closer look at your unique approach to emotions. While we can do so in a lot of different ways, let's start with the simplest: head or heart. Take a look below to see whether your head (those lines on the coloring page) or heart (all that color) tends to be the dominant force in your life.

· · · · · · · · · · · *Head or Heart: 5 Minutes* · · · · · · · · · ·

While we all use both our heads and our hearts,
circle the option on each line that sounds like you *more often:*

○ I prefer facts.	○ I prefer feelings.
○ People are more likely to describe me as logical.	○ People are more likely to describe me as emotional.
○ When someone expresses a strong emotion, I often want to withdraw.	○ When someone expresses a strong emotion, I often try to find a way to engage with them.
○ In conversation, I most often say, "I think. . . ."	○ In conversation, I most often say, "I feel. . . ."
○ I agree more with this statement: "Use your head."	○ I agree more with this statement: "Follow your heart."
○ I grow in my relationship with God most by learning a new truth about him and applying it practically.	○ I grow in my relationship with God most by experiencing him in an intimate way through a personal situation.
○ I find it fairly simple to compartmentalize my life. I can think about one thing at a time.	○ I find it difficult to compartmentalize my life. How I feel affects every area.
○ This is one of my favorite verses: "Do not conform to the pattern of this world, but be transformed by the renewing of your mind" (Rom. 12:2).	○ This is one of my favorite verses: "Trust in the LORD with all your heart and lean not on your own understanding" (Prov. 3:5).

If you circled more items on the left, then your head leads the way for you most of the time. If you circled more on the right, you're a live-from-the-heart kind of girl.

If you're dominated by your head, then you're more vulnerable to avoiding emotions. They may make you uncomfortable and appear to cloud your otherwise clear thinking. You probably don't like being emotional yourself, and you may withdraw when others display emotions as well. You like the facts, just the facts, when you make a decision. After all, what more do you need? This can keep you from being easily swayed. It can also sometimes lead you to miss divine opportunities that don't make sense from a human standpoint. Some of your strengths are likely to be steadfastness, a practical and efficient approach to life, and the ability to stay calm (and bring calm to others) in a variety of situations.

If you're dominated by your heart, then you're more vulnerable to being controlled by emotions. You may jump to conclusions or make decisions without getting the facts you need. You're highly sensitive to others, which helps you be a caring friend and co-worker. It also puts you in danger of "catching" the emotions of others much like someone else might catch a cold. Your emotions can be so strong that when they're in line with God, they can serve as a helpful guide. They may also lead you to assume an opportunity is from him without using wisdom to evaluate it. Some of your strengths are likely to be empathy, a passionate approach to life, and the ability to perceive and respond to the needs of those around you.

Of course, we're all on a continuum. None of us use just our heads or just our hearts. And that's the way God designed it—we're to love him with our hearts *and* minds. The purpose of the exercise above is simply to help you understand which way you naturally tend to lean because it impacts your life, makes you vulnerable in certain ways, and can also be the source of many of your strengths. As we move forward, we'll talk more about who you are emotionally and how you can use that to serve God and others.

How Does God Want Us to Respond to Our Emotions?

Let's talk about that kindergarten class one more time. Imagine a little girl with a coloring book in front of her. Someone taps her on the shoulder and says, "Use this yellow crayon to draw a sun." Then someone else pipes in and says, "No, use this red one to make a fire." A third declares, "You have to make the water blue now!" She may have been coloring contentedly, but now she's unsure. That's often what it feels like when many different emotions try to get our attention. How do we make sure our hearts really reflect what God wants to see?

Fortunately, there's another voice asking for our obedience and attention. It's the voice of the One who loves us. He made the crayons. He created the coloring page. He alone holds the vision for what we're creating with and for him. So what are we supposed to do with all of the other messages we receive? Listen to them, but ultimately obey him.

Emotions make great messengers but bad bosses. If we listen to what the messenger has to share with us, then turn to our heavenly Father and ask, "What do you want me to do?" all is well. If we turn to the messenger with our back to the Maker, then our emotions can lead us astray. While they can share important information with us about our experiences, God always gets the final say.

Peggy, a reader on my blog Heart to Heart with Holley, shared how she replaces the messages emotions give her with the truth from her heavenly Father she really needs:

- Emotion says, "Nobody cares."
- Truth says, "Jesus cares for me."

- Emotion says, "I'm angry and will show her!"
- Truth says, "Be angry and sin not."

- Emotion says, "I'm afraid to hear the doctor's report."
- Truth says, "Fear not, for I am with you."

- Emotion says, "I can't do this anymore."
- Truth says, "My grace is sufficient."[2]

What's Your Emotional Style?

Who we are emotionally grows and changes over time. The little girl in kindergarten is content to express who she is in simple ways. But it won't be long before she trades that box of crayons for boxes of shoes and endless accessories. Instead of creating an image on a page, she creates one for herself. In much the same way, we all develop a unique emotional style—a one-of-a-kind, complex way of showing our hearts to the world as women.

Imagine I pick up you and a friend and take you to your favorite store. As you walk through the door I say, "Surprise! I'm sending you on a shopping spree. You both get to pick an outfit. There's only one rule—it has to reflect *you*." While you and your friend might have a lot in common, you're most likely going to get something entirely different. Maybe you're a "jeans and T-shirt" kind of girl while she heads right over to the pearls and pumps. Even if you choose something similar, you'll probably pick out a different size or color.

What if I took you to another store, but this time it was filled with emotional expressions instead of clothes? The same thing would probably happen. Your friend might feel totally comfortable in bold yellow joy while you feel more at home in the laid-back blue of peace. There would be all kinds of reasons why you made your choices—ranging from where you grew up and what you were taught in church to how your brain is wired.

God, the ultimate designer, has custom created an emotional wardrobe for you. And it's *beautiful*. It's also essential to accomplishing his purpose for your life. So let's explore it together.

The next few sections may feel a little like going into a dressing room. I'm going to ask you some questions, have you try a few things, and give you time to get feedback from your heavenly Father too. We'll find what fits you just right and helps you express the amazing woman he's made you.

The Start of Your Emotional Style

When we look at the trends that come out in fashion each year, they're always new and old at the same time. Designers don't start from scratch. They look back to the past to put a fresh take on the familiar, and usually it works well. When it comes to family fashion, we all know sometimes it's best not to let history repeat itself. Think about that infamous photo where everyone is wearing matching pink plaid outfits for Easter. Enough said.

Since our families are important influencers in our lives, let's start by exploring what emotional hand-me-downs they passed on to us. They might be quality vintage, or it could be time for a new look. This isn't about right and wrong or blaming anyone—it's simply about understanding.

· · · · · · · · · Families and Emotions: 5 Minutes · · · · · · · · ·

Read the descriptions below and then circle the title (Stuffers, Screamers, Surfers) of the one that reminds you most of your family.

Stuffers:

> These families like to keep emotions where they seem safest—on the inside. Have a bad day? Keep it to yourself. Have a really big accomplishment? Settle down. Home is a safe, peaceful place. Please don't rock the boat.

> Wardrobe item: A sturdy, all-season raincoat

Screamers:

> The neighbors already know if you're in a family of screamers. Emotion? Bring it on. Or better yet—bring it

out. Emotions are made to be expressed, not suppressed. Conflict is present and passionate. So is making up. When it comes to emotion, these families are loud and proud.

Wardrobe item: A bright, bold purse that holds a lot

Surfers:

If you're in a family of surfers, everyone just rides the waves. Low tide, feeling a little sad? That's okay—we'll hang out down there with you. High tide, everything fantastic? We can get up to that place and share the joy too. Conflict ebbs and flows naturally. Emotions are just part of life.

Wardrobe item: A pair of shoes that can handle it all—wet or dry

Of course, these descriptions are intended to be lighthearted. They're also stereotypes, so no family fits neatly into one or the other. What's important is recognizing that every family does approach emotion in certain ways that teach us about how we "should" engage with emotion too. Sometimes that's really helpful. Other times it leads us astray. What matters most is recognizing those patterns, testing them against what God says is true, and proactively choosing what to do about them in our lives. Otherwise we just naturally repeat what's familiar.

So let's follow that up with a few more questions about emotion in your family:

In my family, it was okay to feel . . .

(circle three positive and three negative)

○ Afraid	○ Ecstatic	○ Jealous
○ Amused	○ Embarrassed	○ Joyful
○ Angry	○ Empty	○ Lazy
○ Annoyed	○ Encouraged	○ Lonely
○ Anxious	○ Enraged	○ Loved
○ Ashamed	○ Enthusiastic	○ Mad
○ Blessed	○ Envious	○ Overwhelmed
○ Bold	○ Excited	○ Peaceful
○ Bored	○ Exhausted	○ Pressured
○ Brave	○ Fearful	○ Protected
○ Broken	○ Foolish	○ Quiet
○ Calm	○ Forgiven	○ Sad
○ Cautious	○ Free	○ Satisfied
○ Certain	○ Frightened	○ Scared
○ Cheerful	○ Frustrated	○ Shocked
○ Comfortable	○ Fulfilled	○ Shy
○ Compassionate	○ Furious	○ Silly
○ Competent	○ Giddy	○ Strong
○ Confident	○ Glad	○ Supported
○ Confused	○ Grateful	○ Surprised
○ Content	○ Grieved	○ Suspicious
○ Courageous	○ Guilty	○ Sympathetic
○ Defensive	○ Happy	○ Timid
○ Delighted	○ Hopeful	○ Understood
○ Depressed	○ Humble	○ Valued
○ Determined	○ Hurt	○ Weary
○ Disgusted	○ Hysterical	

In my family, it was not okay to feel . . .

(circle three positive and three negative)

○ Afraid	○ Ecstatic	○ Jealous
○ Amused	○ Embarrassed	○ Joyful
○ Angry	○ Empty	○ Lazy
○ Annoyed	○ Encouraged	○ Lonely
○ Anxious	○ Enraged	○ Loved
○ Ashamed	○ Enthusiastic	○ Mad
○ Blessed	○ Envious	○ Overwhelmed
○ Bold	○ Excited	○ Peaceful
○ Bored	○ Exhausted	○ Pressured
○ Brave	○ Fearful	○ Protected
○ Broken	○ Foolish	○ Quiet
○ Calm	○ Forgiven	○ Sad
○ Cautious	○ Free	○ Satisfied
○ Certain	○ Frightened	○ Scared
○ Cheerful	○ Frustrated	○ Shocked
○ Comfortable	○ Fulfilled	○ Shy
○ Compassionate	○ Furious	○ Silly
○ Competent	○ Giddy	○ Strong
○ Confident	○ Glad	○ Supported
○ Confused	○ Grateful	○ Surprised
○ Content	○ Grieved	○ Suspicious
○ Courageous	○ Guilty	○ Sympathetic
○ Defensive	○ Happy	○ Timid
○ Delighted	○ Hopeful	○ Understood
○ Depressed	○ Humble	○ Valued
○ Determined	○ Hurt	○ Weary
○ Disgusted	○ Hysterical	

Imagine we're back in that dressing room, and you're trying on your mama's dress from many years ago. It might fit just right. Or it might need a few changes. And, of course, the most important part is making sure it's in line with what your heavenly Father wants you wearing too. The same is true with our emotions: Much of what we inherited from our families can be good and helpful. But other parts, well, need some altering. And occasionally a piece may need to be tossed out completely.

Every one of us thinks our normal is *the* normal. Our way of life, responses, and, yes, emotions make sense to us. But ultimately, our reality has to be tested against God's ways of doing things. He says, "My thoughts are not your thoughts; neither are your ways my ways" (Isa. 55:8).

- What's one emotional pattern you learned from your family that you want to keep?

- What's one you've outgrown and need to replace with God's way of doing things instead?

Experiences and Our Emotions

We're born into our families, and they influence our hearts from the second we come into this world. As we grow up, experiences also impact our emotional style. The good, the bad, and the ugly all play a role in shaping how we learn to respond to life.

Dr. Ryan Rana, a Christian counselor and friend of mine, says we all have an emotional range. In other words, if emotions are on a continuum, then we've each got a comfort zone. My translation of that range looks a lot like this:

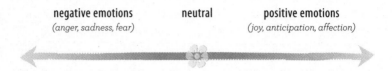

God's intent is for us to appropriately experience the full range of emotions. Even fear plays a helpful role when we encounter a dangerous situation. But often life comes along and we learn that some of those emotions aren't allowed or don't feel safe. In particular, abuse can cause us to narrow our emotional range.

So, Dr. Rana explains, instead of being open to the full continuum of emotions, we may stop ourselves from feeling certain ones. For example, a woman who had a difficult childhood might decide to protect herself by limiting the negative emotions she allows herself to feel. Her range would look like this:

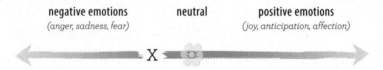

The X represents how far she'll go with those negative emotions. She might let herself experience a little bit of sadness, but not much. Most of the time she keeps it tightly controlled. She thinks, "If I don't let myself have negative emotions, that will keep me safe." But here's what happens:

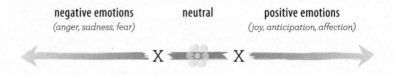

Without realizing it, she's placing an X on the other side as well. When we limit our negative emotions, we limit our capacity to experience positive ones too.

Have you ever tried on a coat that felt too tight—as if you couldn't even lift your arms? That's what we do to ourselves emotionally sometimes.

Now, before you start being hard on yourself if you identified with this example, remember this: at some point in your life, that emotional restriction served a purpose. You probably began it as a child (remember those lists above?). God created in us the ability to adapt and survive our circumstances. Those responses got you through whatever you had to face to where you are now.

It just may be that what once made sense no longer works now. It's time for a new emotional fitting! You may have responses in your emotional closet you "outgrew" years ago. But they're like that teeny tiny T-shirt you've still got from high school—you just can't bring yourself to throw them out.

So, girl, maybe it's time! You are God's beautiful, loved, cherished daughter, and he wants you to live fully. Let's take a look and find some things that fit you just right.

I allow myself to feel . . .

(circle three to five)

○ Afraid	○ Ecstatic	○ Jealous
○ Amused	○ Embarrassed	○ Joyful
○ Angry	○ Empty	○ Lazy
○ Annoyed	○ Encouraged	○ Lonely
○ Anxious	○ Enraged	○ Loved
○ Ashamed	○ Enthusiastic	○ Mad
○ Blessed	○ Envious	○ Overwhelmed
○ Bold	○ Excited	○ Peaceful
○ Bored	○ Exhausted	○ Pressured
○ Brave	○ Fearful	○ Protected
○ Broken	○ Foolish	○ Quiet
○ Calm	○ Forgiven	○ Sad
○ Cautious	○ Free	○ Satisfied
○ Certain	○ Frightened	○ Scared
○ Cheerful	○ Frustrated	○ Shocked
○ Comfortable	○ Fulfilled	○ Shy
○ Compassionate	○ Furious	○ Silly
○ Competent	○ Giddy	○ Strong
○ Confident	○ Glad	○ Supported
○ Confused	○ Grateful	○ Surprised
○ Content	○ Grieved	○ Suspicious
○ Courageous	○ Guilty	○ Sympathetic
○ Defensive	○ Happy	○ Timid
○ Delighted	○ Hopeful	○ Understood
○ Depressed	○ Humble	○ Valued
○ Determined	○ Hurt	○ Weary
○ Disgusted	○ Hysterical	

I don't allow myself to feel . . .

(circle three to five)

○ Afraid	○ Ecstatic	○ Jealous
○ Amused	○ Embarrassed	○ Joyful
○ Angry	○ Empty	○ Lazy
○ Annoyed	○ Encouraged	○ Lonely
○ Anxious	○ Enraged	○ Loved
○ Ashamed	○ Enthusiastic	○ Mad
○ Blessed	○ Envious	○ Overwhelmed
○ Bold	○ Excited	○ Peaceful
○ Bored	○ Exhausted	○ Pressured
○ Brave	○ Fearful	○ Protected
○ Broken	○ Foolish	○ Quiet
○ Calm	○ Forgiven	○ Sad
○ Cautious	○ Free	○ Satisfied
○ Certain	○ Frightened	○ Scared
○ Cheerful	○ Frustrated	○ Shocked
○ Comfortable	○ Fulfilled	○ Shy
○ Compassionate	○ Furious	○ Silly
○ Competent	○ Giddy	○ Strong
○ Confident	○ Glad	○ Supported
○ Confused	○ Grateful	○ Surprised
○ Content	○ Grieved	○ Suspicious
○ Courageous	○ Guilty	○ Sympathetic
○ Defensive	○ Happy	○ Timid
○ Delighted	○ Hopeful	○ Understood
○ Depressed	○ Humble	○ Valued
○ Determined	○ Hurt	○ Weary
○ Disgusted	○ Hysterical	

When we look in the Bible, we see the full range of emotions—especially in the Psalms. David expresses everything from wild joy to deep sorrow. *And all of those honored God.* Remember what we talked about earlier? It's what we do with our emotions that matters. For example, "In your anger do not sin" (Eph. 4:26).

So give yourself permission to feel and to find the right "emotional fit" for your heart.

It's okay to be sad.

It's okay to be happy.

It's okay to be mad.

I'm not talking about "venting" the way the world often tells us we need to do. God clearly wants us to use self-control through his Spirit and show love to those around us when we're expressing our emotions. If we're emotionally restricted or numb because of our wounds *or* if our emotions are wildly out of control, it's a sign that something is broken within us.

If that sounds like you, especially if you've experienced abuse, I recommend seeking help from someone you trust like a counselor or mentor. It can take time and a listening ear for our emotions to heal and for us to be comfortable with them again.

Then when you're ready, step out of the dressing room and give those emotions a twirl.

Emotional Evidence

It's one of the great mysteries of womanhood that we all have moments when we stand in our closet, look at our clothes, and still think, "I've got nothing to wear." And I've got a confession: it's been one of those weeks for me emotionally. Of course that would happen when I'm writing this chapter! I'm not dressed up but I've got someplace to go—a big ol' pity party. You know the kind where the theme song is, "Nobody likes me, everybody hates me, I'll just go eat worms"? Yep, that's been me the last few days.

Tonight as I sat on the couch moping, this thought crossed my mind: *Your emotions have nothing to do with reality right now.*

It caught me off guard (in case you haven't figured it out, I'm a live-from-the-heart kind of girl, and I tend to take what I feel at face value). But the more I considered it, the more I realized it was true. Now, there have been weeks when my emotional state would have been appropriate because it would have been a response to something that had happened. That wasn't the case this time. My circumstances and emotions were vastly different. When that happens, it's time for an emotional style reality check.

Imagine you're back in that dressing room and I'm one door over. I slide on that neon pink self-pity dress that caught my eye on the rack. I tell you as I step into the hall, "Oh, I have a feeling this is going to look *good*." Then we both turn to the mirror, and it looks like I've been hosed down with Pepto-Bismol. You know what I'm talking about, don't you? Our emotions are like that sometimes too. We think what we feel is right and real. But then we take a closer look and find we couldn't be further from the truth.

The higher you scored on "Heart" in the first section, the more likely this is to happen to you. But we're all susceptible to being caught up in emotions that are nothing more than a mirage at times.

As I thought more about my pity party, the Israelites came to mind—especially the story of Joshua and Caleb (see Num. 13–14). You remember that one, don't you? Let's all have a quick review together. The Israelites have been trekking across the desert to the Promised Land. They've seen miracles galore, and God has provided for them. He's also said, "This land is your land—go get it! And by the way, it's *good*." So they send up some spies to check it out. Sure enough, it's a wonderful land beyond their wildest imaginations. But there are also giants in the land. The spies (except Joshua and Caleb) come back and say, "Sure, it's great. But there's no way we can defeat those folks. We should just give up." Joshua and Caleb step up and say, "No way! God gave this land to us. And he'll give us the victory we need too!" You know the rest of the story. The naysayers win out, and the Israelites wander in the wilderness for forty years.

We all have a point at which we have to choose which evidence to believe. Do we rely on our emotions alone? Or do we look into God's truth and let him tell us what's real? Fear won that day in the desert—and an entire generation paid the consequence. Only Joshua and Caleb lived to actually see the Promised Land.

Faith is more important than emotion. Again, I'm not talking about the "fake it until you make it" or "grin and bear it" approach to emotions. The Israelites having those emotions in the desert wasn't the issue. It was that they chose to obey their fear rather than God's command. At the end of the day, we've got to listen to and follow God's Spirit more than our own hearts. He's the ultimate reality check. We also need sisters of faith who will speak truth to us when we can't see it or simply don't have the strength to believe it in that moment. Seek out "Joshuas and Calebs" who will do more than just go shopping with you—they'll make sure you get to the Promised Land too.

The Most Important Accessory for Your Emotional Style

In those moments when we look in the mirror of truth and realize our emotions aren't lining up with reality (that little pink self-pity dress is a disaster waiting to happen), what can we reach for instead?

Thankfully, God promises to give us something better to wear. And it's just right for our calling in life. We're not going to prom, ladies. We're going to a battlefield. That's why he tells us to guard our hearts, and he's given us the perfect outfit to do so. We each have a unique emotional style. But no matter what that may be, God still wants to give us just the right accessories. And they complete it, *complete us*, in a way that's powerful and beautiful.

Finally, be strong in the Lord and in his mighty power. Put on the full armor of God so that you can take your stand against the devil's schemes. For our struggle is not against flesh and blood, but against the rulers, against the authorities, against the powers of this dark world and against the spiritual forces of evil in the heavenly realms. Therefore put on the full armor of God, so that when the day of evil comes, you may be able to stand your ground, and after you have done everything, to stand. Stand firm then, with the belt of truth buckled around your waist, with the breastplate of righteousness in place, and with your feet fitted with the readiness that comes from the gospel of peace. In addition to all this, take up the shield of faith, with which you can extinguish all the flaming arrows of the evil one. Take the helmet of salvation and the sword of the Spirit, which is the word of God. (Eph. 6:10–17)

While all of these armor accessories are important, one stands out above the rest: the breastplate of righteousness. That's because it's the one that covers the heart. And that's really what we've been talking about all along. "Above all else, guard your heart, for everything you do flows from it" (Prov. 4:23). All of this talk about emotions matters because our hearts affect *every other part of who we are and what we do.*

At first I didn't understand why righteousness would be what covers our hearts. But then it became clear: *choosing to do what is right in spite of our emotions protects us.* Think of times in your life when you've let your emotions get the best of you. I'm recalling some now, and the first word that comes to mind is "ouch." Exactly. When we let our emotions get out of control, we get hurt. And often others do too. When God says, "Obey me rather than your emotions," he's really looking out for our best interests.

But it seems like a tall order, doesn't it? Choosing what's right regardless of how we feel is no easy task (at least for me—maybe

I'm the only one). So I dug a little deeper into this idea of guarding our hearts, and that brought me to this Scripture: "Do not be anxious about anything, but in every situation, by prayer and petition, with thanksgiving, present your requests to God. And the peace of God, which transcends all understanding, *will guard your hearts* and your minds in Christ Jesus" (Phil. 4:6–7, emphasis added).

Worry is a sign that we're letting our emotions get the best of us. (And believe me, I know. When it comes to worrying, I'm a pro.) So when we start sensing those feelings taking over, God invites us to come to him instead. When we say thanks along with our requests, we're reminding ourselves of what's true regardless of the circumstances at the moment (remember Joshua and Caleb?). God says that then his peace, which is beyond all understanding, will guard our hearts. It's like a bulletproof vest that looks gorgeous too. Simply stunning.

Stepping onto the Red Carpet of All God Has for You

On the show *What Not to Wear*, Stacy London and Clinton Kelly surprise women with wardrobe makeovers. At the end of each episode, the woman gets to say a few words about her experience. Almost all of them express something like this: "I feel freer to be who I am and pursue my dreams." Many also add that they feel beautiful for the first time.

I'm sure none of you need a wardrobe makeover (although if you'd like to nominate me, please go for it!). But I do hope our little journey leaves you feeling much the same way. God made you an emotional being. That's a beautiful, powerful, glorious thing. After all, the reason we have emotions is because God has them too. We read in the Bible about him feeling everything from anger to sadness to joy. We have the capacity to reflect him through our emotions because we're created in his image—every part of us. Those tears you cry. That smile you give. The anger you express at injustice.

God has given you a wardrobe of emotions fit for a princess because that's what you are in his eyes. Wear them royally, with your heart held high, and show the world what it means to be a passionate woman who has the courage to truly experience life and express herself (and the One who knows her heart best) with love and grace through it all.

I'm imagining a car pulling up to the curb.

You step out of it, confidently placing your feet on the red carpet of God's plans for you.

I wave wildly, snap a picture, and smile from deep inside.

Oh, girl, your heart is looking fabulous today.

5

Where Am I Going?

My car came with a GPS (global positioning system). Despite its best efforts to get me from one place to another, the phrase I most often seem to hear is, "Make a U-turn if possible." My husband somehow set it to the British version, so it sounds a bit like I'm being reprimanded by Mary Poppins all the time—quite distressing. I'm still hoping they'll come out with a Southern version that says, "Now, honey, it sure seems like you've had a rough day. Why don't you pull on over and get yourself a nice, big mocha?"

But for now it's Ms. Poppins and I zipping down the road together. Whenever she starts giving me directions, the first thing I do is look for the little red dot on the screen that represents my car. It essentially tells me, "You are here." After all, before we know where we're going, we need to understand where we are at the moment, right?

We've just spent time in the last chapter getting all dressed up in our emotional style. And as every girl knows, the next step when you're all dressed up is to find somewhere to go—and then get there quick. But it seems when I don't pause first to be certain I know where I am, that's when I get myself into the most trouble. I turn too soon or pass up an intersection, which leads to frustration and even discouragement. Thinking we're one place in life when we're actually somewhere entirely different can derail us from being the amazing women we are and doing what we're called to do. So let's pause and look for that dot.

When I think about the journey of our lives, of course the first thing that comes to mind is when God took the Israelites from Egypt to the Promised Land. You remember that, don't you? The Israelites had been in slavery for hundreds of years. God sent Moses to tell Pharaoh to let the people go. Through a series of miracles, the Israelites were finally free and began their journey through the desert to the wonderful land God had for them. And all along the way, God himself was their divine GPS!

Although I'm sure God did a much better job than my "Mary Poppins," the Israelites still ended up doing more than their share of wandering around too. Like for me, a lot of that happened because they just couldn't grasp where God had them at the moment and hang on to that truth in the middle of their circumstances. As they say, if you can't be an example, be a warning. So take it from the Israelites and from me that things work out better when you know where you are and where God wants you to go.

As I looked at the story of the Israelites again, I wondered how they knew when to stay put and when to move along. It turns out the answer is right there in the middle of the story:

> Whenever the cloud lifted from above the tent, the Israelites set out; wherever the cloud settled, the Israelites encamped. At the LORD's command the Israelites set out, and at his command they encamped. (Num. 9:17–18)

The cloud above the temple was God's presence. So to sum all that up, *wherever God went, the Israelites went too.* He asks us to do the same in our lives. Our role is not to rush ahead but instead to stay right by his side.

That means we're going to have different phases of our lives. Sometimes we'll encamp and sometimes we'll set out. We'll take a closer look at what that means soon. But first, let's have a little heart-to-heart about why this is so hard for us as women.

The Road Less Traveled Is Always the One You're on Right Now

Remember how we talked about our tendency to compare? That doesn't just apply to our strengths—it often extends to where God has us in life. We think, "I need to volunteer for every committee at church because Susie does and she's so godly." Or we might tell ourselves, "I need to quit every committee at church because Anna did and she's so peaceful." We feel like we need to do more, less, or something entirely different than everyone else. We end up zigzagging from spot to spot on the map and wear ourselves out in the process. All the while God is saying, "Dear daughter, I'm here, right here. Won't you join me?"

Here's the good news: God has a journey for *your* life. It looks different than anyone else's. The road he's carved out for you is yours alone. It's always the road less traveled because you're the only one who is ever going to walk it. Oh, sure, he'll give you wonderful traveling companions to go with you. But don't let that fool you: that doesn't mean their paths are the same as yours—just that they're parallel for a time.

So if you've been feeling guilty that your path doesn't look like Spiritual Samantha's then breathe a deep sigh of relief. Your GPS (God Positioning System) is going to get *you* exactly where you need to go. And he promises to be with you every step of the way.

With that said, there are some common stops along the way in our journeys. The Israelites experienced them too. Taking a closer look at those can help us accurately place our "You are here" dots and give us a better understanding of those places.

Keep in mind that where you are in different areas of your life may vary. For example, professionally you might be in the Promised Land while personally you're feeling like you're in the desert, or vice versa. If you relate to several of the spots below, that's totally normal, and I'll give you a tool to help you map them all at the end.

When You're in Egypt

We all begin our journeys in the same spot the Israelites did—Egypt. Most biblical scholars believe that Egypt, a place of slavery, represents how we're all born into sin. We're controlled by it. Then God comes along and promises to set us free.

If you're a Christian, you don't live in Egypt anymore. If you haven't started a relationship with God yet, you can do so right now by giving your life to him. Just tell him something like this:

> God, I believe that you exist, that you love me, and that you sent your Son to die on the cross for my sins. I ask your forgiveness for those sins, and I receive your gift of a right relationship with you and eternal life in heaven. All I am and all I have is now yours. Amen.

Once we make that commitment, our address is no longer in Egypt because God has set us free. But we can sometimes find ourselves in that old place again. Let me be clear: I'm not talking about your salvation. Once we belong to Jesus, "our citizenship is in heaven" (Phil. 3:20). But we may end up back in Egypt for a visit. That happens when we let sin take over our lives again.

You know that feeling, don't you? Instead of moving toward what God has for you, it seems you're going backward. Your life feels out of control. It might be because of an addiction, a destructive relationship, or a pattern you just can't break. Whatever it is, you don't have to stay in Egypt! If you've given your life to God, you're his always. Sometimes we just need to stop and realign with his direction for our lives again. You can start that by praying something like this:

> Lord, thank you that I am yours and that you have a plan for my life. I've gotten off track and ended up in Egypt again. Please forgive me. I want to make a U-turn right now. I want to be where you are and live in your presence. Help me change. Amen.

Egypt is a powerful place, and we often need the help of others to get free. Have you ever gotten your car stuck in the mud or seen someone else do so? The wheels endlessly spin, but there's no forward motion. Usually the only way to get the car out is to have someone else pull it onto solid ground again. If you're feeling "stuck," then find someone you can trust—a friend, spiritual mentor, or counselor—who can help you get back on the road. There's no shame in that, girl. We've all been there and will most likely go there again. His grace is your highway out of Egypt and on to better things. As Karen, a reader on my blog *Heart to Heart with Holley*, powerfully declared, "The same God who delivered me from the sins of my past will deliver me from the sins of my present!"[1]

· · · · · · · · · · · · *Am I in Egypt? 5 Minutes* · · · · · · · · · ·

Is there an area in my life where I feel like I'm in Egypt?

- ° In bondage
- ° Out of control
- ° Oppressed
- ° Separated from God's presence

If so, what area is it?

° God, I want out of Egypt. Please help me to

° Someone I trust and can confide in about this is

And I have promised to bring you up out of your misery in Egypt into . . . a land flowing with milk and honey. (Exod. 3:17)

When You're Encamped

I always wondered how the Israelites could have taken so long to complete a journey that turned out to be about eleven miles. What were they doing all that time? It turns out much of it was spent encamped. In other words, God just told them to stay put for a while. As long as the cloud stayed over the tabernacle, they remained in camp:

> When the cloud remained over the tabernacle a long time, the Israelites obeyed the LORD's order and did not set out. Sometimes the cloud was over the tabernacle only a few days; at the LORD's command they would encamp, and then at his command they would set out. (Num. 9:19–20)

Okay, ladies, it's time for a little confession. I don't do well with being encamped. I'm a "let's get on the road" kind of girl. Yes, ma'am. Pack up those tents, put them in the car, and let's go! And yet there have been multiple times in my life when God's direction to me has clearly been the worst four-letter word of all in my vocabulary: *wait*.

As I look back over those times, I can see that waiting was indeed part of the overall plan and served a purpose. There are many reasons why God may tell us to encamp for a period of time. For the

Israelites, it was an extended "time-out" because they'd blatantly rebelled against God. But that's not always the case. And trust me, if that's why you're waiting, you'll clearly know it. So let's take a closer look at some of the other reasons why God may have us "encamp" for a while.

~ *We're Weary* ~

Making progress in life is hard work. When we insist on moving forward as quickly as possible, we can wear ourselves out in a hurry. Sometimes when God makes us wait, it's one of the most merciful things he can do. It doesn't inherently mean we've done something wrong. In fact, it can indicate just the opposite—that we're right between some really big things God has for our lives, and we need to rest up.

Let's talk about another biblical story we probably all know, from 1 Kings 18. It's one of my favorites because I'm a Texas girl and this is the original showdown. I'll set the scene: Elijah is a prophet of the Lord who challenges the prophets of Baal to prove who's the real God. Everyone shows up. The prophets of Baal make an altar and ask their god to bring down fire on it. Nothing happens. Elijah does the same, and fire comes down in an astounding way. It's an unmistakable victory.

So what does Elijah do next? He hightails it out of town, sits under a tree, and says, "I have had enough, LORD. . . . Take my life" (1 Kings 19:4). Then he falls asleep. So God strikes him with a bolt of lightning. The end.

You'd think that would make sense, right? Nope, that's not what happened. Instead God sends an angel to take care of Elijah, to feed him and make sure he gets even more rest. Then the angel says, "Get up and eat, for the journey is too much for you" (1 Kings 19:7). After that meal, Elijah has the strength to travel for forty days. At the end of that time, God shows up in Elijah's life in another powerful way.

God knows we're human. He knows we get worn out. Sometimes he simply says, "Take a break, child." I have friends with young kids, and naptime doesn't ever seem to be very welcome. The kids almost always protest. But in the end, my friends make sure their little ones get the rest they need for their own good. We can be like those reluctant kids too. We're so set on getting where we want to go that the last thing we want to do is nap (or encamp). But our heavenly Father, in his infinite tenderness, knows that sometimes that's exactly what we need most.

~ We're Healing ~

As I began to write this section, I glanced up at the wall. A plaque just above me reads, "As for God, his way is perfect" (Ps. 18:30). It shows a peaceful path between tall trees. I leaned back in my chair and sighed a bit, relieved at the reminder that God's ways are perfect—but mine don't have to be. And they never are. One of my favorite songs talks about how God blesses the broken roads of our lives.

Life's hard. We get hurt. That means sometimes what we need most is for God to stop us right in the middle of our road as we limp along and say, "Daughter, sit down. Rest. Heal. Let me tend to your wounds."

After a particularly painful season in my life, I walked into the bathroom at an office and burst into tears. My emotions caught me off guard. I had been telling everyone I was just fine! As I found a quiet corner to process things for a moment, Jesus seemed to show up right beside me. Later that day, I wrote this about it on *Heart to Heart with Holley*:

> Hot tears slam my cheeks, slide down, rivers of unbidden emotion.
>
> I'm shocked at their appearance—hot lava exploding from a mountain that had just been covered in daisies.

I slip into a bathroom stall, place my head in my hands, sniffle into a square of paper. That year . . . *so good,* so hard.

I felt more like a warrior than a writer.

My heart has the scars to prove it.

But then, softly, a whisper comes, "Put down your sword."

And I notice, for the first time, how my heart has stood in ready-to-fight position for so long, stiff, waiting to dodge the next blow.

I relent. And something inside clatters to the ground. I see the wounds, still fresh, not noticed in the heat of the battle. I touch them tentatively. Cover protectively.

Then again, softly within . . .

"If I will wash your feet, will I not wash your wounds?"

I have a choice. *Drop my guard or guard my hurts.*

I choose the first.

And His hand touches all that aches, His voice whispers truth, His love wipes *around, over, down.* It stings a little. I flinch with old fear. But slowly I relax, lean into Him, remember the time before the war, and I know it is finished.

No longer a warrior.

I'm a child, small, safe, with Daddy's hands making it all better.

Victory.

Surrender.

I leave the bathroom stall, finally, look into clear eyes in the mirror.

And I am never the same again.

. . . .

We want to move forward in our lives. We want to keep saying "I'm fine" and pressing ahead as if that's really true. But Jesus, in his infinite love for us, sometimes slows us down for a season so that he can heal our hearts.

∼ *We're Being Prepared* ∼

I have a new obsession: the Food Network. I know, I know—it's not the deepest thing out there. But in a time when things feel a little chaotic in life, it's wonderful to know that sugar, flour, and eggs in the oven at 350 degrees predictably do what you intend.

But before that can happen, there's a lot of preparation. Whole shows are built around it. Rachael Ray, Paula Deen, and others talk to the audience while slicing, dicing, mixing, and stirring. Imagine an episode where they skipped all of those steps.

It might sound like this: "Hey, y'all, today we're baking Make-You-Gain-a-Dress-Size Mango Muffins. I'm in a little bit of a hurry, so instead of mixing and measuring, we're just going to put the whole bag of flour and sugar right in the oven and see what happens."

I imagine the results might not help the ratings! Yet I often approach God's purpose to my life the same way: "Hey, God, today I'm really ready to get to the next phase of my life. You know, the one where everything is wonderful? So I think I'll just mix some unfulfilled desires with quick fixes, throw in some steps taken in my own strength, and see what happens."

Whoopsie. It doesn't usually turn out quite like I had in mind.

God's plans for our lives take preparation. That's not my favorite part—I just want to get to the end result. But sometimes God asks us to "encamp" so that he can do the necessary work in our lives for his purposes. Then when the time is right, we get to dig in and enjoy!

∼ *It's Just Not Time Yet* ∼

Ladies, I know none of us like this, but it's just got to be said: sometimes *it's just not time yet.* There's no logical explanation for the delay. God is simply doing his thing. "'For my thoughts are not your thoughts, neither are your ways my ways,' declares the LORD" (Isa. 55:8).

When this happens in our lives, the enemy tries to slip in and tell us all sorts of nonsense. For example, "If you were a better person, then this would have worked out by now."

My friend Julie Sawyer Philips has walked this path. For years, she prayed to be a wife and mom. Finally, the first request was answered. Although she and her new husband applied to adopt a child, nothing seemed to be happening. During that time, they had the opportunity to have dinner with the daughter and son-in-law of the couple who ran the orphanage where they had applied. With all of them having busy schedules, only one particular day and time would work.

When they finally got together, the couples took time to pray and asked God to bless the child he had for John and Julie. Four days later, the phone rang and a voice on the other end said, "We have a baby boy for you!" When Julie considered the time difference, she realized her new son had been born the very same day those prayers were offered. During the years Julie had been "encamped," God had been working out every detail. She said with a broad smile on her face, "Isn't that amazing? I can tell my son there was never a moment of his life when he didn't have a family."

You may be "encamped" in a way you don't understand either. God offers this hope: "He who began a good work in you will carry it on to completion until the day of Christ Jesus" (Phil. 1:6). In other words, whatever journey God begins in your life and heart, he promises to finish—in his perfect timing.

∼ *Whatever the Reason...* ∼

Ecclesiastes 3:11 says, God "has made everything beautiful in its time. He has also set eternity in the human heart; yet no one can fathom what God has done from beginning to end." That verse speaks to what it's like to be in the mysterious middle—of circumstances, of unmet expectations, of the journey from Egypt to Home. When we're in the "middle" of life, we can take comfort in knowing we're right in the center of God's hands too.

If you feel "encamped" in your life right now, it may be for any of the purposes we talked about above. Whatever the reason, use this time to rest and receive the truth your heart needs for the journey. You are loved. God has a purpose for you. He is working out his plans for your life.

And just when you least expect it, you'll be on your way so he can take you all the way to the Promised Land.

· · · · · · · · · · · *Am I Encamped? 5 Minutes* · · · · · · · · · · ·

Is there an area in my life where I feel like God is asking me to "encamp"?

- Waiting
- God may seem silent
- Doors aren't opening for me to move forward
- I feel the need to rest or heal

If so, what area is it?

- God, sometimes simply staying where we are is difficult. Please help me to

- Someone I trust and can confide in about this is

> The LORD replied, "My Presence will go with you, and I will give you rest." (Exod. 33:14)

Setting Out

Encamping doesn't last forever, and when the cloud of God's presence lifted, the Israelites knew it was time to move. When God does the same in our lives, we may have several responses. Which one sounds most like you?

◦ **The Settler**
"What? Set out? I'm quite content right here. I just got things the way I want them. You go ahead and maybe I'll join you later. Change is pretty scary, after all."

  • Strengths: Good at maintaining security and peace. Willing to stay with something as long as it takes. Faithful and trustworthy.
  • Areas for growth: Tends to view change, even when it's from God, as negative. May get stuck in a rut and refuse to move forward.

◦ **The Explorer**
"Bring on the change! I'll race you to the Promised Land. I may not be sure where I'm going, but I'm making good time. Life's an adventure and new is fun."

  • Strengths: Willing to take risks and go in a different direction. Moves forward and often helps others do so as well. Embraces and encourages change.
  • Areas for growth: Sometimes takes risks or tries new things for the experience rather than being led by God. May put tasks ahead of relationships for the sake of progress.

◦ **The Traveler**
"I'm packed and ready to go. I feel a little uneasy, but I'm still willing to take the next step. We'll see what happens. Life is just as much about the journey along the way as it is the destination."

  • Strengths: Takes life in stride and tries to move at the pace of God and others. Flexible and adaptive. Interested in what is ahead but doesn't rush to get there.

- Areas for growth: Sometimes can end up wandering longer than necessary. May be indecisive or too easily sidetracked by others.

We each play these roles at some point in our lives, but one is probably your natural tendency. And this is never more apparent than when God says, "It's time to set out!" By understanding how we normally respond to change, we can pause and be sure we're really doing what God wants and not just what's most comfortable for us.

We can also ask ourselves the following questions when it's time to take a step or make a change.

～ *Am I Being Led or Driven?* ～

Sonic is a popular fast-food restaurant in the South. Home of the infamous cherry limeade, it's also reminiscent of the days when carhops brought food to you. One afternoon I pulled in, and as I waited for my order to come, I glanced at the car next to me. A toddler about two years old was perched in the driver's seat with his little hands wrapped around the wheel and a look of determination on his face. I laughed out loud since the car was safely in park and he was right in the middle of his mama's lap.

As I thought more about that scene and how it seemed oddly familiar, I slowly realized I was a lot like that toddler. I wanted to grab the steering wheel of my life and zip down the road. It seemed God gently whispered to my heart, *"If you're driven, you can't be led."* I knew in that moment that me being in charge of my life wasn't any wiser than that little boy driving down the highway. God in his mercy was letting me know that I could take a seat on the passenger side and he'd gladly get me where I needed to go.

We can be driven by all kinds of things—fear, insecurities, ambition, pride, comparison, or lies from our childhood. But we can only be led by one Person. Jesus promised the Holy Spirit would lead us into all truth (see John 16:13). Instead of God's presence being a cloud above the temple, we have God's presence within us. "Your body is a temple of the Holy Spirit" (1 Cor. 6:19 NIV 1984).

The next question naturally seems to be, "But how can we know if it's the Holy Spirit leading us?"

First, simply begin to make a habit of asking God to speak to you and then listening for his voice in your life. As you do, make sure what you hear lines up with God's Word—anything that's from him always will. Also ask for guidance from others you trust. "Surely you need guidance to wage war, and victory is won through many advisers" (Prov. 24:6).

Then take a step. Sometimes the step you take won't be exactly right, and that's okay. "Many are the plans in a person's heart, but it's the LORD's purpose that prevails" (Prov. 19:21). Ask God to redirect you as needed. Learning what God wants for our lives is a process. As the book of Romans says, we're to "test and approve" God's will (12:2). In other words, if God is asking you to set out, then sometimes the only way to know is to go!

~ Is My Pace Matching God's? ~

Like we talked about earlier, we all approach change differently. If you're a Settler, you may tend to go a bit slower than God might want at times. If you're an Explorer, you may race ahead. God wants us right by his side. And when we are, the journey doesn't wear us out, and we even find joy along the way.

One morning my husband and I set out for a bike ride. A brilliant blue sky hung above us, and the first kiss of fall found its way onto our cheeks as we began to zigzag down the trail. Biking hasn't always been easy for me (okay, it never has). I do enjoy it—especially on flat pavement. But we live in a hilly part of the country, and every ride is full of ups and downs (anyone else feel a spiritual analogy coming on?).

My husband is a great biker, and my big breakthrough came when he taught me how to use my gears. You see, I had been doing everything in the hardest gear. I was showing off, really. I thought if I could tackle the biggest, baddest hill in that gear, then I must be good.

But that's just silly. And I understood why when I learned you can make it easier to pedal just by a little flick of your fingers. Now my gear fits the terrain. I can adapt, shift, and make the most of where I am at the moment.

When I find just the right gear, it almost feels like flying.

God has been giving me some "gear lessons" in the rest of my life the last few months too. Just like I am on my mountain bike, I tend to be a bit intense in my spiritual life. I think, "I'll just do it all in the hardest gear. That will prove what a good little Christian I am." Can anyone say "craziness"? But now, instead, the One who loves me is gently showing me how to shift, adapt, and allow seasons of rest between seasons of pushing hard. It's changing everything for me.

What pace do you tend to go? What gear do you tend to use? When we take time to align ourselves with God's pace and purposes, our journey suddenly feels different. As Isaiah 40:31 says, "But those who wait on the LORD shall renew their strength; they shall mount up with wings like eagles, they shall run and not be weary, they shall walk and not faint" (NKJV). It's clear from those words that this kind of waiting isn't passive—it's more about keeping pace with God.

And when we do? Well, it almost feels like flying too.

∼ *Am I Making God My Ultimate Destination?* ∼

Think of a trip you took with someone you love. Maybe it was a family vacation, a honeymoon, or a way to celebrate a milestone. While you may have gone to a beautiful place, the best part of all was probably the relationship.

When God asks us to set out, we can get so focused on moving forward, on getting to the Promised Land, that we forget that the real point of the journey is our relationship. Yes, God moves us forward, but most of all he simply wants *us*.

It can seem hard to believe at times, but it's true—the God of the universe wants to share life with you. Every step. Every day. All the way to your forever home with him.

· · · · · · · · · · *Am I Setting Out? 5 Minutes* · · · · · · · · · ·

Is there an area in my life where I feel like God is asking me to "set out"?

- An urge to take the next step
- God seems to be speaking and guiding
- Doors may be opening for me to move forward
- I'm sensing the need for change—even if it's hard or uncomfortable

If so, what area is it?

- God, it seems you're asking me to "set out" with you. Please help me to

  _____

  _____

- Someone I trust to walk with me through this is

  _____

  _____

> *Have I not commanded you? Be strong and courageous. Do not be afraid; do not be discouraged, for the L*ORD *your God will be with you wherever you go. (Josh. 1:9)*

The Promised Land

After we escape from Egypt, do some camping, and move forward when God says to, then we finally make it to the Promised Land.

For believers, heaven is the ultimate Promised Land. But God gave the Israelites a Promised Land in this life as well. I believe he often does the same for us too. Let's define a Promised Land as this: *a desire of your heart that God guides you into through an intimate journey with him.* Maybe you were single for years and God brought along your husband. You might have been trying to have a baby and suddenly you saw the bright pink "yes" of that line on a pregnancy test. Perhaps you got the position at work you'd waited so long to get. Or your health returned after a struggle with illness.

All of our Promised Lands look different. And because we live this side of heaven, none of them are perfect. We'll still disagree with that husband God gave us, grow a little weary of changing diapers for the baby we wanted so badly, or realize this job has more responsibilities than we bargained for when we asked for it. But even in the middle of all that, we know this is where our hearts belong.

Also, we won't make it to all of the Promised Lands our hearts long for this side of heaven. We live in a fallen, broken world, and some of the desires of our hearts will only be met when we cross from here to eternity.

Sometimes we become so sure that we won't make it to our Promised Land in this life that we're taken by surprise when we do. Or perhaps we've been so intent on getting there that we're not quite sure what's next when we actually arrive. After my husband and I reach a destination and set down our suitcases, the first question out of one of our mouths is usually, "What should we do now?" We pull out a guide to the area and make a plan.

After all the praying, waiting, and moving forward, it's time for us to explore what God has given us too. Fortunately, he gives us a guide to use as well. So what does he say we're to do when we get to our Promised Land?

～ *Possess It* ～

When the Israelites arrive at the edge of the Promised Land, God tells them to go in and make it fully theirs. He asks us to do the same too. That can take a lot of hard work and fighting some battles. Possessing the Promised Land isn't a one-time event but instead a process.

> *God's Guide:* "The LORD your God will drive out those nations before you, little by little. You will not be allowed to eliminate them all at once, or the wild animals will multiply around you" (Deut. 7:22).

Like Joshua and Caleb, we're to believe that the Promised Land will ultimately belong to us, but the way that actually happens usually takes time and courage on our part.

～ *Defend It* ～

As the years went by, the Israelites drifted away from their faith in God and eventually were exiled from the Promised Land for many years. When we get to where God is taking us, it doesn't mean we can get so comfortable that we let our guard down or neglect our relationship with him.

> *God's Guide:* "Be careful that you do not forget the LORD your God, failing to observe his commands, his laws and his decrees that I am giving you this day. Otherwise, when you eat and are satisfied, when you build fine houses and settle down, when your herds and flocks grow large and your silver and gold increase and all you have is multiplied, then your heart will become proud and you will forget the LORD your God, who brought you out of Egypt, out of the land of slavery" (Deut. 8:11–14).

While the Israelites did have to fight the nations around them, the biggest threat ended up being from within. Gratitude and obedience are the best defenses for our Promised Land.

~ *Enjoy It* ~

Once we're in our Promised Land, God wants us to enjoy it! After wandering in the wilderness so long, our joy muscles can get a little weak. Give yourself permission to celebrate where God has brought you and what he has entrusted to you.

> *God's Guide:* "The LORD your God is bringing you into a good land—a land with brooks, streams, and deep springs gushing out into the valleys and hills; a land with wheat and barley, vines and fig trees, pomegranates, olive oil and honey; a land where bread will not be scarce and you will lack nothing; a land where the rocks are iron and you can dig copper out of the hills. When you have eaten and are satisfied, praise the LORD your God for the good land he has given you" (Deut. 8:7–10).

· · · · · · · **Am I in the Promised Land? 5 Minutes** · · · · · · ·

Is there an area in my life where I feel like God has brought me to the Promised Land?

- A desire or prayer answered
- A sense of being where I belong
- Renewed joy and anticipation
- Passion to possess and defend what's been given to me

If so, what area is it?

- God, thank you for bringing me to the Promised Land. Please help me to

---

- Someone I can celebrate this with is

> *When you have eaten and are satisfied, praise the LORD your God for the good land he has given you. (Deut. 8:10)*

· ·

Your Life Map

The Israelites' divine GPS guided them every step of the way and eventually got them to the Promised Land. God promises that if we follow him, he'll do the same for us too.

Let's think back to my little GPS—the one in my car that we talked about in the very beginning. I mentioned how I "zoom in" to the little red dot representing my car because it helps me know where I am and where I'm going. We've been doing the same for your life.

One more way I use my GPS to stay on track is to "zoom out" so I can get the full view. Then I see that little red dot in the full context of where I am and where I'm going next. Because our lives are complex, we actually have more than one dot. As I said before, you might be in one place personally and someplace totally different professionally. That's even more reason for us to step back and see the big picture.

To tie everything together, let's build a map of where you are in different areas of your life. Take a look back over your answers in each section of this chapter and use them to fill this in:

• • • • • • • • • My Life Map: 5 Minutes • • • • • • • • •

Under each section draw a dot and write the areas of your life that fit in each one.

Egypt

Promised Land

Encamped

Setting Out

Where do you have the most dots? They might all be clustered in one area right now, or you may literally be "all over the map"!

By knowing where you are in life, you can ask God for what you need in each area. You can also let others in your life know how they can come alongside you. Perhaps most important, you can give yourself grace by understanding that these are stops along the way. You won't be where you are forever. God promises that when you trust him, he'll take care of you wherever you are and get you where he wants you to go.

In the meantime, I'm going to step in and pretend to be your personal GPS for the day. Here's what I'm saying to your heart: "Way to go, girl! You've made a lot of progress in this chapter. Now pull over and celebrate because God has you headed somewhere good. He's given you all you need and made you exactly who you need to be for your journey. He'll get you where he wants you to go in his perfect timing."

6

Who's **with** Me?

The women gather, laugh, hug, and reconnect. I stand at the back of the room. I ask the silent questions we rarely dare to speak aloud.

Will I fit in?

Will anyone like me?

I'm at a conference. I know many of these women. I've met some in person and connected with others online. We call each other friends, support each other through hard times, cheer each other on . . .

And yet.

Insecurity pushes me into the corner. I become a wallflower, not growing but wilting in the feeling of being alone right in the middle of a crowd.

Eventually the feeling passes.

But I know it will come again.

I think we all experience this as women. We're part of families. We join churches. We do bunco in our neighborhood or join the school board. We are on Facebook, send emails, write cards to one another.

We know what it's like to be connected and yet feel alone.

Throughout the journey we talked about in the last chapter, we look to our left and right, our hearts asking the question, "Who's with me?"

Of course, the Sunday school answer is "God."

And that's true—God promises to always be with us.

Yet it seems he also created within us a deep desire to share life with each other—flesh and blood. In the Garden of Eden he declared, "It is not good for the man to be alone" (Gen. 2:18). It's not good for women either. We need others to speak truth to us, remind us we're amazing, walk alongside us, and encourage us in all God has called us to do.

We may tell ourselves, "If only I were closer to God, I wouldn't feel like I needed other people so much." But Adam lived in a perfect place. There was no sin. He had an intimacy with God we can only imagine. Yet God still said that Adam being alone wasn't good.

So that ache you feel, that longing you can't name? You don't need to feel guilty about it. It's the magnet God places within you that draws you to other people. It's part of his plan. *It's good.*

When God says being alone is "not good," the contrast is stark. Remember the seven days of creation? After sky, water, birds, animals, light, and dark, God says, "It is good." And yet now he is announcing the opposite. A life without relationships with other human beings isn't good—isn't what he planned.

In today's world of going-it-alone, pull-yourself-up-by-your-bootstraps thinking, it often seems we disagree. Oh, perhaps it's not stated directly. But even in churches it sometimes feels as if needing other people is a sign of weakness.

If only my relationship with God were stronger, then I wouldn't be lonely.

If only I could get my act together, then I wouldn't care at all what other people thought.

But wanting other people in your life isn't weakness. Instead it's a reflection that you are created by a God who is inherently relational. Look at the lengths he's gone to just to have a relationship with you.

Why was Adam being alone not good? *Because it's not like God.*

Father.

Son.

Holy Spirit.

The kingdom we serve in is one of love, relationship, and intimacy. We're not made *for* each other, but we're certainly made to share life *with* each other.

What You Have to Offer as a Woman

As the daughters of Eve, being made to share life with others is especially true of us—it's central to what makes each of us amazing. God created Eve with relationships in mind. When we think of Eve being created as a "helper" for Adam (Gen. 2:18), we tend to assume that word describes her role. But what if it's much deeper than that? What if it describes her heart?

Think of the women in your life. Encouraging, comforting, cooking, painting, working . . . it's almost all for someone else. They labor on behalf of love. This "helping" varies in its intensity. Sometimes it's a soft hand brushed across the hot brow of a sick child. But often it's fierce, strong, wild, bold.

The word for "helper" is the same word often used when God helps us. David uses it in the Psalms: "We wait in hope for the LORD; he is our help and our shield" (33:20). Here the help that comes from God is the kind one needs in war—it stands side by side with a shield.

We, as women, often do go to battle. We fight cancer. We fight for our marriages. We fight for our children. And in doing so, *we help*.

Perhaps we have defined this word too narrowly because a part of us grasps what it truly means. Deep inside we have sensed our full calling . . . and it frightens us. So we define, and let it be defined for us, that "helping" is quiet and safe.

And sometimes it is. It has been said that humility is "strength under control." So at times we do help in the ways servants do—not because we must but because our hearts love deeply enough to put the needs of others before our own. This is a beautiful part of being a woman.

But other times, perhaps, we hold back our help because it would mean stepping out of our comfort zones and getting messy, dirty, and involved. We know it would take all of our strength, we might get wounded in the process, and people could misunderstand.

Yet it remains that we are "helpers" created and called by the One who is our help. So we must look to him for the complete picture of what that word means. God's heart is the place where "woman" began, and though we may look elsewhere, it is still the place where we (as women) find who we are in the end.

The world needs you as a woman to do what only you can do, to love the way only you can love, to offer what you have to share.

Believe me, sister, it's beautiful and worth much more than you can even imagine.

Why We Hold Back

If we have so much to offer, why is it so hard to open ourselves up? What keeps us from fully giving ourselves in relationships? After connecting with thousands of women, I've discovered several common reasons—all of which I can personally relate to as well.

We're Afraid We Won't Be Loved

I pull jeans from my closet and hold them up to the light. I'm about to fold them neatly into my suitcase when I notice the rough cuffs.

I grab scissors and snip at loose ends. They only fray more. I tug and pull. (Did I mention these are my *good* jeans?) I sigh and lean back against the wall. And as I do, I realize my jeans aren't the only thing with frayed edges.

My heart has them too.

I shouldn't be afraid of this trip. I'm looking forward to seeing old friends and making new ones, to learning and time with Jesus.

And yet (confession coming) a part of me still feels insecure.

Fear pulls at the edges of my heart.

My jeans are frayed.

And I am afraid.

Neither of us seems quite good enough at the moment.

And as I stand there, jeans still in hand, a change begins to happen. It seems Jesus lays his hands on those frayed edges, those places I wish were different, and he stitches them up with grace. He tells me again,

- Love all. Please One.
- Be who I've created you to be.
- You are enough because I am enough in you.

Each line is like a thread that mends something inside me. I run my thoughts along those frayed edges of my heart, amazed—they suddenly feel smoother and more whole.

And my jeans?

I put them in my suitcase.

I decide I'll just wear them anyway.

I'm slowly learning it's not about being perfect but about being perfectly loved.

"There is no fear in love. But perfect love drives out fear" (1 John 4:18). This verse has come to mind over and over as I've thought about relationships and why they're so hard for women. We strive for perfection, after all. It seems like the ideal insurance policy against rejection, doesn't it? If our house, habits, and heart are just right, who wouldn't love us? And yet all the time we know that we aren't perfect, that we won't ever be this side of heaven. Round and round it goes until God stops us as he did me that day with my jeans and tells us again, "Beautiful daughter of mine, you don't need to be perfect. You are already perfectly loved."

The hard part is translating that into our relationships. Perhaps we can grasp that God loves us, but it seems more uncertain that our friends or family are likely to follow suit. I recently pondered that, and it seemed God whispered to my heart, "There is no fear in love—if you are acting out of insecurity, then you are not living in love." That hit home.

I protested, "But God, I want people to like me. I want people to be happy with me. Isn't that what it means to be loving?" And as I dug deeper into his Word it became clear that, no, being loving doesn't mean pleasing people. *We are to love people, but we're only asked to please God.* "Am I now trying to win the approval of human beings, or of God? Or am I trying to please people? If I were still trying to please people, I would not be a servant of Christ" (Gal. 1:10).

We're called to care about others, to be kind and considerate, to try our best to bless them. But, ladies, we don't have to make everyone happy. *And if we don't have to make everyone happy, then we don't have to be perfect.* God has already declared us good enough, worthy in his sight, valuable, and with much to offer the world.

Please listen to this: if you are loving toward others and following God's will as best you can and someone else talks negatively about you or rejects you, then they are responsible to God for that sin. Yes, it's sin for someone else to gossip about you, criticize you to others, or cut off their relationship with you in an unloving way. *And you are not responsible for the ungodly responses of others.*

If others have wounded you in this way, I'm so sorry. I'm asking God right now to heal those hurts, to release you from the burden of feeling it must have been your fault and from the endless striving of trying to make things right—or to be just right.

I used to walk on eggshells around other people, say yes when I wanted to say no, and worry endlessly about what someone might whisper behind my back if I didn't please them. Then I realized that they're accountable to God for their words and actions. If I'm doing my best to be loving, God says, then others are to come to me and tell me if I've offended them. (The same works in reverse—others are not responsible for pleasing us either.) And we're to guard our lips against criticizing them or gossiping about them as well. We're not here to please each other. We're here to please the One who put us on this earth.

So if you've felt afraid to put yourself out there because you feel less than perfect, because you're afraid what others might say, then reach out your hands and open your heart, sweet sister. You are already perfectly loved, and you only have to please the One who has already declared you are a delight to his heart.

We Only Feel Safe When We're Hiding

Adam and Eve forget their purpose is to please God. They fall, then hide. But God doesn't let them stay there. He finds them again.

Hide-and-seek. Our hearts have been playing that game ever since.

Every kid has their favorite hiding places. Mine were under my brother's bunk bed, behind an old chair in the garage, and in the laundry basket (how I fit in there, I'll never know). What were yours? At first hiding was fun. But at some point, I just wanted someone to come get me.

As a child, I hid physically. As an adult, I'm more like Adam and Eve. My insecurity makes me hide emotionally. God asks my heart, "Why are you hiding?" On any given day, the answer varies:

- Insecurity.
- Perfectionism.
- Hurt.

But his response is always the same—to call me back to confidence in him, remind me of who I am, and bring me back into the light of his love.

God seems to prefer *seek-and-find*. "You will seek me and find me when you seek me with all your heart" (Jer. 29:13).

Here's how it works: we come out of hiding, and then we're free to pursue God's heart, chase his will, freely follow his path for our lives. I remember how as a child playing hide-and-seek, one person would eventually yell, "Olly olly oxen free!" I still have no idea what that means, but it seems God makes the same declaration to our hearts: it's safe to come out of hiding. In the game of life, we're free, loved, found forever.

We don't have to hide in our relationships with others either. As we talked about earlier, we're called to love those in our lives, but we don't have to please them. The hardest part is having the courage to live that way—to stand in the open rather than hiding.

While God does want us to be open with others, he also encourages us to put boundaries in place as we do so. He talks repeatedly about guarding our hearts. So what's the difference? *Hiding is a response out of fear, while guarding is a proactive choice to protect what matters most.* In other words, we're not to deliberately put something of worth where it won't be valued. Some people in our lives can't or won't treasure our hearts. In those cases, it's okay to limit how we share ourselves with them. What God wants us to avoid is making a habit of hiding that leaves us feeling alone and as if no one really knows us.

· · · · · · · · · · · · *Safe Person Checklist* · · · · · · · · · · · ·

How do you know if someone in your life is safe? The short answer: if they love you the way God does. First Corinthians 13 gives us a checklist. No one does this perfectly, including us! What we're looking for is someone who tries to love this way, even if they mess up at times.

A safe person...

- Practices patience
- Treats you with kindness
- Finds joy in your blessings and success
- Stays humble
- Considers your needs
- Gives unselfishly
- Is slow to become angry
- Doesn't hold grudges
- Defends you
- Trusts you
- Hopes for the best
- Sticks with you no matter what

Let's look at the opposite of that list too.

An unsafe person...

- Frequently gets impatient
- Treats you unkindly
- Envies you
- Is prideful
- Doesn't take you into consideration
- Takes whatever they can get
- Quickly becomes angry
- Holds grudges
- Wounds you
- Is suspicious and untrusting
- Believes the worst
- Abandons you when you need them most

The first list is how God intends for you to be loved—and how he wants you to love others too. If you've experienced or expressed anything else, it's not from him. Find the people in your life who will love you like this, and forgive the ones who can't or won't. Broken people have sharp edges, and you may have been deeply wounded. If that's what's driven you into hiding, then God wants to set you free to feel safe and to love again.

It may seem scary to think of being in relationships with others, of coming out of hiding. Jesus knows what it's like to live in this world. He knows what it's like to have someone you love betray you, to be abused, to be crucified when you're innocent. *He knows.* And he still says, "Love is worth it."

Coming out of hiding doesn't mean that we won't ever get hurt. We will. It doesn't mean people won't disappoint us. They will. But it does mean that we'll be able to love and be loved, to experience life the way God intends—with each other.

And God will help us guard our hearts. "He is my loving God and my fortress, my stronghold and my deliverer, my shield, in whom I take refuge" (Ps. 144:2). God wants to be your protection.

Oh, sweet sister, it's been hard hiding, hasn't it? It's exhausting, lonely, scary. God wants to whisper to all of our hearts, "Come to me. Stand with me. I will be with you. I will go before you. I will be your shield. You don't have to carry the burden of protecting yourself anymore. I'm here. I love you—and I want you to experience the love of others too."

Drop that mask. Tear down that wall. Step out from behind that barrier. *Dare to love.*

We've Got to Have Control

Sometimes it seems the best way to protect our hearts is to have control. Relationships are messy, after all. Unpredictable. We know if we put cookies in the oven and bake at 350 degrees for a certain amount of time, the results will be what we want. But if we put love into our lives and circumstances turn up the heat, we're not sure what may happen.

We've talked a lot about Eve and how as women we're still impacted by that one important choice she made in the Garden. Ultimately, that choice was about control. Eve wanted to "be like God, knowing good and evil" (Gen. 3:4). While it may hurt to admit, many of us want the same—especially in relationships.

Control can usually be traced back to one emotion: fear. We want to feel safe. And the only way to feel safe is to know what will happen. The only way we can know what will happen is to be sure we're in charge of it, right?

As a counselor, I see many of my clients struggling with issues of safety and control. It often leads to anxiety and depression in their lives. Naïvely, I assumed I didn't struggle with control because I had little desire to tell others what to do. But in his loving-kindness, God slowly began to peel back the layers of my heart and reveal that, yes, I did struggle with control too. My attempts to control just looked different. Instead of controlling others, *I controlled myself.* I set unrealistic expectations for my behavior. I put standards in place that were impossible to meet. I wanted to be perfect—which would be the ultimate display of control.

I began to realize there are two primary ways we tend to approach control as women. Both impact our lives and relationships.

~ If you're drawn to external control... ~

- You want to determine the behavior of others
- You are often tempted to be critical
- You may be seen as "bossy"
- You have high expectations for those in your life
- You feel unsafe in situations in which you can't determine the outcome
- You're drawn to positions of power

∼ *If you're drawn to internal control...* ∼

° You are very strict with your own behavior
° You are quite hard on yourself
° You tend to be anxious and find it difficult to relax
° You have high expectations of yourself
° You feel unsafe in situations in which you don't know what others expect
° You are continually pushing yourself to do and be more

All of us struggle with control in both of these ways at times, but there's usually one tendency we're drawn to more than others. (I also want to be sure to clarify that this kind of self-control is different than what the Bible talks about. Self-control as a fruit of the Spirit is a natural outflow of God leading our lives. It's ultimately God-control. The kind of control we're talking about here is self-imposed so that we feel safe.)

It's easy to read what's above and be hard on ourselves about it. But picture for a moment yourself as a little girl. You fear monsters under the bed, so you keep a little light on every night. You're not sure what's in that closet, so you never open the door. You hear a noise in the dark and insist your mom stays with you until you're asleep. We're not little girls anymore, but we still know that life can be full of darkness, "monsters," noises we don't understand, things that make us feel afraid. So we cope. *We control.*

Give that little girl inside of you some grown-up grace. Tell her you know she's scared and you're sorry she doesn't feel safe. Then tell her about the heavenly Father. The One who is the forever light, who loves her, who promises to keep her secure no matter what happens.

Notice I said "secure" and not "safe." Because the reality is that life and relationships *aren't* completely safe. Jesus said, "In this world you will have trouble" (John 16:33). We will get hurt. We will face loss. We will be disappointed. It seems as if control is a cure for this—but it's only an illusion. It traps us tight within our fears. Freedom only comes when we find security in Jesus, when we realize that life is hard but he is good and *no matter what happens* he'll get us through it. Life is risk. Love is risk. As C. S. Lewis said:

> To love at all is to be vulnerable. Love anything, and your heart will certainly be wrung and possibly broken. If you want to make sure of keeping it intact, you must give your heart to no one, not even to an animal. Wrap it carefully round with hobbies and little luxuries; avoid all entanglements; lock it up safe in the casket or coffin of your selfishness. But in that casket—safe, dark, motionless, airless—it will change. It will not be broken; it will become unbreakable, impenetrable, irredeemable.[1]

Control keeps us alone. God invites us instead to love—to that wild, unknown, heart-pounding reality of relationships. We're to give him the reins of our hearts, and then he loves others through us. Are you ready to let go of a little control and let more love into your life?

Learning to Love

Once we've faced all the reasons we might be holding back our hearts, then the question becomes "How do I build relationships?" The answer to that question is as unique as you are. Just as God has given you specific strengths and skills, he's also created you to connect with others in particular ways.

As women, we can struggle with feeling we have to be "all things to all people." We look at Chatty Cathy and wonder why we're not more outgoing. We listen to Deep Debbie and feel like we should be more insightful in talking about our faith. We squirm in crowds and feel safe one-on-one. Or just the opposite. Usually we simply sigh and ask, "Why do I act this way?" The beautiful answer to that question just may be, "Because that's exactly how God made you, sweet girl."

When we think about the biblical command to "love one another," it seems like the way we go about doing so should be one size fits all. But the way God expresses his love through you will look entirely different than the way he does it through someone else. *And that's good.*

So let's explore how he wired you, *amazing you*, to be a reflection of his love.

7

How Do I Connect?

Imagine we're on a playground. One feisty little girl leads her peers in a spontaneous game. Another talks quietly with a friend in the sandbox. Both seem utterly content in the way they connect with others.

Then we grow up and learn words like *outgoing* and *shy*, and the labels make us squirm. When certain social situations make us feel uncomfortable, we tell ourselves we shouldn't feel that way. We pile on the guilt for not being "loving" and try harder. But the truth still remains—particular ways of connecting with others feel as natural now as they did back when we were those kids on the playground.

What if God made us that way? What if he wired our social tendencies just like he did our other strengths and skills? Perhaps the way you connect with those around you is just as needed as the other gifts in your life. Maybe it's even at the heart of what makes you amazing.

Your Social Strengths

As we talked about in the last chapter, God is relational. And I believe he formed each of us with certain ways of reaching out to others. So let's take a closer look at what that means for you in the following sections. (And yes, they all start with *S* because I'm an alliteration addict and just can't help myself.)

These are general categories. They're intended not to box you in but instead to help you do a little exploring. We're all complex, unique individuals, and there's no way to fully capture who we are in a few sentences. So use these tools in whatever way is helpful to you. Follow them completely as they are, make up your own, or somewhere in between. They aren't absolutes—just ways of thinking about who we are and how we connect. God knows you better than anyone, so also ask him to be your partner in this process and show you what you need to know about who he's made you.

Also, even within the category that fits you there will be variations between you and someone else who chose the same one. We're all on a continuum and have our own spot. Just treat these as starting places and adapt them to wonderful, one-of-a-kind you.

Setting

Amanda slips into the party. Her palms feel sweaty and her knees knock a little. There are so many people! She glances over at her friend Molly who's loudly telling a story and has an entire group laughing. "Why can't I be more like her?" Amanda wonders. She drifts across the room and spots her friend Sarah in a quieter corner. She quickly grabs the chair next to her and settles in for a long chat. It turns out Sarah has had quite the week and really needed an empathetic ear in the middle of all the chaos. Amanda has always been a great listener. As she tunes out the crowd, her racing heart slows and she feels comfortable again.

You have a dominant social setting preference. One way to recognize it is by asking yourself what you usually choose if you have an evening free to do anything you'd like with others. Do you plan a party? Have dinner with a few friends? Make time for a long chat over coffee with just one person?

Your answer gives you a glimpse of who you are and how you relate to others. Which of the descriptions below sounds most like you?

One-to-One:

You prefer situations in which you can focus intently on an individual. You listen carefully and seek to offer your full attention. Your conversations are likely to have depth, and you want to hear what's really going on in the other person's life and heart as well as share the same. While you enjoy people, you probably don't have the desire for an extensive inner circle. That would require spreading yourself too thin. After all, a relationship is a significant, serious investment that requires the best of you.

In a group of people, you may feel overwhelmed or frustrated that you can't give each person the attention you'd truly like. You also may have little patience for small talk and chatter, seeing them as a distraction from what matters most. You have a strong capacity to make people feel truly valued and heard.

One-to-Few:

You are drawn to situations in which you can be in a close circle of people. Most often, those in that circle are people you already know. You feel safe and comfortable because you have history and an understanding of who is around you. You don't necessarily need to have deep conversations because you know so much about each other, although you can do so at times. You enjoy hearing how each person approaches life and learning from them. You also like seeing how each individual engages with the others in different ways. You are a peacemaker and relationship maintainer.

You don't necessarily mind meeting new people but don't naturally go out of your way to do so and may avoid situations completely if people you know aren't going to be there. You know how to talk as well as listen and can do so with one person or the whole group as the conversation flows. You make people feel comfortable and as if they belong.

One-to-Many:

You thrive on groups of people. You have a seemingly endless capacity for connection. While others might be intimidated by having lots of people around, you are excited by the opportunity. You could be called a "social butterfly," and you often act much like one—flitting from person to person with ease.

Most of your conversations are more casual because you need to spread your emotional energy around, although you can go deeper if someone really needs you. If someone takes too much of your time, you may start feeling trapped. You're able to lead, speak in front of a group, or coordinate many people if needed. You love seeing how different people are, and there's no such thing as a stranger to you—just another friend waiting to be made. You make people feel included and help them engage in life and with each other.

Of course, we're all going to experience each of the settings above at different times. Understanding our preference doesn't mean we avoid the others. But it's important to know because the one that fits closest with you is where you'll have the most to give to others. If you're more of a one-on-one girl, then you might want to consider being a life coach. If you're one-to-many, then that leadership position in women's ministry might be a really great opportunity for you.

You can also get rid of the guilt you feel for not feeling equally comfortable in all of these situations. It doesn't mean anything is wrong with you—it's simply how you're wired. For the sake of others, we choose to be in situations out of our comfort zones. But that doesn't mean we have to feel ecstatic about it. God made you to love others in your own wonderful way.

Which one sounds most like you?

◦ My strongest social setting is:

Structure

Pam stands in front of a microphone and smiles at the women in front of her. This conference has taken months of careful direction and planning. Now the day has finally come and everything is in place. Well, almost. She notices someone has forgotten to put coffee in the back. Pam makes a quick mental note to ask for that to be taken care of before the first break. Then she takes a deep breath and welcomes the women for the day. She knows it's up to her to set the tone, and she's up for the challenge.

Now that we've looked at which settings you're drawn to with others, let's talk about the structure of those relationships. There are three primary relationship structures: leading, partnering, and following/serving. Depending on where you are (work, home, etc.) these may vary for you. But there's usually one that you naturally gravitate to more of the time.

If you made graphs of each of these they would look like this:

Leading	Partnering	Serving
You		Others
↻	You ⟷ Others	↻
Others		You

Leading:

If you prefer the leading structure of relationship, then you're confident being in charge. You enjoy setting direction and inspiring others to join you on the journey. Those in your life likely listen to you and look to you for advice. When you're not depending on God as your ultimate leader, you may come across as controlling. But when you're being directed by him, you have the ability to take many people to places God wants them to go and to guide them well along the way.

Partnering:

If you're drawn to the partnering structure of relationship, then you view everyone in life as your equal. You want to be side by side or face-to-face. You see connecting with others as an endless process of give-and-take. You care little for power but don't want to be taken advantage of either. You may become agitated by issues of balance and fairness. You have a strong capacity for coming alongside others and encouraging them, sometimes simply by your presence through whatever they face. You believe we're all better together.

Serving:

If you fit closest with the serving structure of relationship, then you see humbling yourself as the best way to lift others up. You're willing to do whatever is needed and offer support without resentment or envy. You likely feel uncomfortable with the spotlight and avoid attention. You may sometimes use service as a way to make yourself feel needed or earn love rather than giving freely and confidently. If you find a worthy leader, you are quite content being a follower. You're a strong, steady support and gain joy from helping others in the journey of life.

Which one sounds most like you?

- My strongest social structure is:

Sight

Alison and Meg have been best friends for years. Although their lives are busy, they try to make time for lunch every few weeks. When they get together, it usually goes the same way. Meg stops to talk to at least three people she knows before she makes it to the table. She sits down commenting about the changes in the décor or the weather outside. She asks Alison, "How's it going? What have you been up to?"

Alison looks a bit startled when Meg suddenly bursts onto the scene, interrupting her thoughts. She smiles and tells Meg a little bit about the new idea she has for a project at work. She thinks Meg seems a little more tired than usual. She mentally runs through the reasons why that might be the case. Then she asks, "Meg, how have you been? How are you feeling?"

When it comes to life, we all have vision that's stronger in particular areas. Just as our eyes can be nearsighted or farsighted, we see more clearly in certain social situations. In this case, it doesn't need to be corrected—it simply needs to be recognized and maximized. When you do so, your way of seeing the world can become a strength.

There are two primary types of sight when it comes to relationships: external and internal.

External:

> If your social sight is externally focused, then you're highly tuned in to your environment and the people in it. You notice details about the ones you love. You remember events in their lives like birthdays. You are aware of what's going on with them and take the time to show it. When you're in a conversation, you have the ability to watch facial expressions and body language while staying aware of your surroundings too. You're likely to ask "How's it going?" and really want to know what's happening in the lives of others. You show love in tangible, often practical ways.

Internal:

> If your social sight is internally focused, then you are highly tuned in to the unseen world that exists around you and within those you love. You seem to intuitively understand what others are feeling or thinking, often without them telling you so. You are more likely to live in the realm of the heart. When you talk intently with someone, the rest of the room frequently fades away. You want to know the passions, desires, and dreams of those you love. You express that you care in ways that are invisible but still deeply meaningful—listening, speaking encouraging words, and silently providing support.

Of course, all of us can pick up on the external and internal cues around us. What this really describes is your primary focus in relationships.

Which one sounds most like you?

◦ My stronger social sight is:

Sphere of Needs

Jill, Tina, Kris, and Valerie all sign up to go on a mission trip at church. A few months before they are to leave, they get together to do some planning.

Jill starts out by saying, "The most important thing is for people to know about the need. So many people don't even realize what's happening in that country! I'll put together a newsletter we can send to our friends and family."

"That sounds great," replies Tina. "I've been reading some of the stories and it seems like so many of the women in that place are just really hurting. I just want to go so I can listen, cry with them, and make sure they know how much they're loved."

Kris chimes in, "I think what matters most is just being there to spend time with people so we can build relationships—and continuing that even when we're back home. Our presence is what's really going to make a difference."

"And I've got big plans while you're doing that," says Valerie with a smile. "I'm bringing an extra suitcase with all kinds of food that I've been collecting. You can find me in the kitchen! I think the best way to feed a hungry heart is to feed a hungry mouth first."

When you use your social sight to focus on others, needs begin to appear. And of course you want to meet them. The needs that stand out most to you and the ways you feel compelled to fill them for others are the final aspect of your social strengths.

We can think of needs this way:

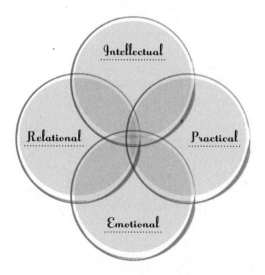

While we're called to help meet all of these needs in the lives of others at various times, and they often overlap, there's likely to be one or two we're especially called and equipped to fulfill.

Practical:

> If you're drawn to meet the practical needs of others, you're likely to see what needs to be done and then do it. You use your hands to meet needs—whether that is cooking, setting up, writing a check, or making something happen

in a tangible way. You feel satisfied when you see actual results from your giving.

Emotional:

If you're wired to meet the emotional needs of others, you offer your heart first. You know when someone is hurting or desires to have someone rejoice with them. You give through intangible ways most often—comforting, encouraging, bringing hope. You don't need to see actual physical results from the way you give other than a smile appearing or a tear being wiped away.

Relational:

If you desire to meet the relational needs of others, then you see your presence as the best gift you can offer. You show up whenever it matters most—in the hard times as well as the happy. You may not even talk about what the other person is feeling or be compelled to take a specific action. You simply want to be there for support, to share the experience, and to be a connector.

Intellectual:

If you focus on the intellectual needs of others, you're likely to try to connect them to truth first. You might offer to pray for them right away, share a helpful Scripture, or pass along a book that offers wisdom for their situation. You want others in your life to know what matters most because you believe it impacts every area of their lives.

You may wonder why there isn't a category labeled "spiritual." That's because I believe all of these are spiritual. Jesus said if we even give a cup of cold water to someone in his name, it matters and will be rewarded (see Matt. 10:42).

Also, as believers Jesus wants us to meet all kinds of needs in the lives of others. This is intended not to get us off the hook for serving in other areas but instead to help us see where we're probably called to give more of the time. If you could only do one of the categories above, which one would you pick? That's your primary sphere of needs, but stay open to serving in other ways as well.

Which one sounds most like you?

° My strongest sphere of needs is:

_____

_____

Why Does All of This Matter?

We often try to force ourselves to be like others or to simply do whatever we're asked. Then we wonder why we feel ineffective and exhausted. We are the body of Christ—and that means we not only have individual strengths to offer; we also have unique ways of loving others. Of course, sometimes we'll need to step outside of those for a special need or season. But knowing how we connect lets us serve in the center of the way God made us.

For example, if you're someone who circles one-to-one, partnering, internal, and emotional, then you would probably make a great counselor. But you'll likely feel frustrated as a youth worker taking forty teenagers on a mission trip to build a house. In contrast, if you circled one-to-many, leading, external, and practical, then that same trip is likely to thrill you.

So how do you make the most of who God has made you to be? Here are a few thoughts that apply to your social strengths as well as all the other strengths we've talked about along the way too.

Stay in Your Strengths When You Can

Sheila just started a new job. Through her previous work, she learned that she's very good at leading teams on projects. When she attends a meeting about an upcoming initiative, she wants to volunteer to be the team leader. It even seems a little voice inside whispers, "Fear not, for I am with you." But she's worried about not being good enough, so when it's time for assignments, she takes the task of working with one other person to record all the data collected during the project. Her co-worker

Debbie is made team leader by default. At that news, Debbie's face turns pale, and she mutters something about "feeling overwhelmed."

A few days later, Sheila stops by Debbie's office. It's clear her co-worker is upset, and Debbie confides again that she really wishes she didn't have to lead the team—she'd be much better at taking care of the practical task of collecting data with the other co-worker. Sheila breathes a sigh of relief and confesses that she too has been struggling with her part of the project. She whispers a prayer, "Thank you, Lord, for second chances." They meet with their manager later that day and make a plan to trade roles. Months later the project is successfully completed, and both women feel energized about taking on the next challenge.

I recently helped facilitate a study, and one section focused on using our gifts. At the end, a woman stood up and said something along the lines of, "If we try to meet the needs of others in ways God is not asking us to, then not only are we likely to burn out—we're also taking the place of whoever really is supposed to be meeting that need."

Yes, sometimes women use "that's not my strength" as an excuse to get out of a legitimate opportunity for service. But more often than I see them ducking out of what God is asking them to do, I see women taking on roles and responsibilities because they want to please people, they feel obligated, or they simply assume that's the "Christian" thing to do. If that's how you've been feeling, then give yourself permission to serve first in those areas that are in line with who God created you to be and how he designed you to love. *He'll rejoice, and we'll all benefit.*

> The body is not made up of one part but of many. Now if the foot should say, "Because I am not a hand, I do not belong to the body," it would not for that reason stop being part of the body. And if the ear should say, "Because I am not an eye, I do not belong to the body," it would not for that reason stop being part of the body. If the whole body were an eye, where would the sense of hearing be? If the whole body were an ear, where would the sense of smell

be? *But in fact God has placed the parts in the body, every one of them, just as he wanted them to be.* (1 Cor. 12:14–18)

No one can take your place. God doesn't have a "plan B" for you. You have gifts to offer the world, ways of connecting that only you can fulfill.

Here's the thing: God's not the only one with a plan for your life. The enemy has one too. And if he can't get you to rebel outright, then sidetracking you and getting you outside of your strengths is a pretty good alternative. Convincing an ear it needs to act like a hand is sure to limit its effectiveness, right? Your strengths are worth protecting. You are of incredible worth to the kingdom. Dare to be who you are—who God created you to be.

When You Need to Step Away from Your Strengths, Have a Strategy

"Hey, Candace, it's Molly. I'm checking with all of the moms in the classroom to see if they can help with the bake sale in March. Are you free that day?"

"Sure, I can make some cookies."

"Actually, we have all the baked goods taken care of already. We really need someone to work at the booth and talk to the other parents."

Candace takes a deep breath. She's much more comfortable in her kitchen than being the meet-and-greet mama. She senses a hesitation inside.

"Listen, Molly, I really do want to help. Can you just give me until tomorrow and I'll let you know for sure?"

"Sure," replies Molly. "That would be great. Thanks for considering it—talk to you later."

Candace hangs up the phone and whispers a prayer. "Lord, do you really want me to do this, or is it just a distraction?" She's learned that before stepping outside of her strengths, it's important to take time to pray. By the next day, she feels like she's got her answer.

She picks up the phone again—but she's not calling Molly yet.

"Amy? This is Candace. I know how good you are at talking with all the moms at school and the way you love a crowd. Will you be my bake sale buddy?"

Candace tells Molly the good news that she has two volunteers for the day. During the bake sale, Amy and Candace make a great team with Amy doing most of the talking and Candace ringing people up. Candace also loves the moments in between the busy times when she can spend some one-on-one time catching up with her friend.

It's often when we step outside our strengths for a season that we learn and grow. That's a necessary part of becoming all God wants us to be. But it's still important to have a plan. My husband and I like watching the travel channel. As soon as the guide on the show announces she's going into unknown territory, all kinds of preparation starts taking place. Clothing gets changed to adapt to warmer or cooler weather. Gear gets packed. Maps are pulled out. Because of that work, the trip usually turns out to be enjoyable. But imagine the guide said, "I live in Hawaii and today we're going to Alaska in the middle of winter. I'm sure what works here will be just fine there too." Then we'd fully expect to see chattering teeth and a very unhappy camper by the end of the episode.

In much the same way, we can find joy in any circumstance. But it always takes prayer and usually some strategic planning to make sure that happens when we're crossing the borders of our strengths into other territory.

Even if we do have a strategy, we're not intended to stay outside of our strengths for the majority of the time. Our strategy can act like a sunscreen for a little while, but we can't live out on the beach twenty-four hours a day—even if it seems wonderful at first—and not get burned. Like that travel guide, don't be afraid to step outside your strengths for a visit when God asks you to do so. But be sure to get yourself back home in the end.

Always Be Led by the Spirit

Karen strides into the room, thinking, "Oh, I've totally got this. They're going to be eating out of my hand in no time."

Wendy follows behind her, thinking, "There's no way I can do this. I'm just going to keep quiet and leave as fast as I can."

Whether we're talking about strengths or weaknesses, the biggest temptation is to rely on ourselves. When that happens with our strengths, it shows up as arrogance and pride. When it's our weaknesses, it leads to insecurity and shame.

Jesus invites us to a better way. He says we don't have to go through life in our own power anymore. Instead he promises that when we belong to him, the Holy Spirit comes to live within us. The Spirit is many things to us—a guide, a comforter, a counselor, and the One who leads us into all truth. He's the every day, every moment companion of our hearts.

The Spirit enables us to live the way God wants and to be all he's created us to be. "For God did not give us a spirit of timidity, but a spirit of power, of love and of self-discipline" (2 Tim. 1:7 NIV 1984).

- *Power*—We don't have to live in our strengths on our own. The Spirit is the One who enables us to do what we're called to do.
- *Self-discipline*—Even in the times when we don't feel like obeying, the Spirit will help us do God's will.
- *Love*—Whatever God wants us to do is ultimately about love, and the only way we can love like he does is through the Spirit within us.

"Being led by the Holy Spirit" can sound vague or super-spiritual. But it's really just moment-by-moment, day-by-day dependence. It's acknowledging that even in our strengths, we need a lot of help. And even in our weaknesses, God can enable us to do more than we imagined. We're amazing not because of who we are but because of who lives within us.

What Matters Most Is Love

Even when we live in our strengths, love still requires sacrifice. Jesus said that if we're going to follow him, we need to take up our cross and deny ourselves. The point is that it's *our* cross—not someone else's. Jesus didn't say, "Take up your cross and deny who God made you." The part of ourselves that we're called to deny is the sin nature within us that wants its own way. We're never to use our strengths (or weaknesses) as an excuse for being selfish. Instead we're to see all of who we are as an invitation to serve. "You, my brothers and sisters, were called to be free. But do not use your freedom to indulge the flesh; rather, serve one another humbly in love" (Gal. 5:13).

I'm thinking of you as I write these words. I imagine you with your head bent over this book, maybe with a highlighter in your hand, on your couch, in the passenger seat of a car, or on a plane. I'm wishing more than ever that we could have coffee today. I'd tell you, "You are loved. You matter. You have so much to give the world and the hearts in it."

Let's dare to love, to share life with each other, to offer ourselves in the way God has created us to do.

I need you.

You need me.

The kingdom needs *us*.

8

What Does God Want Me to Do with My Life?

I curl up on a chair in the corner of my bedroom. I hold a cup of coffee in one hand and my journal in the other. I've come with questions for Jesus.

I run my fingers along the fabric of the chair. It's almost fifty years old—an heirloom from my grandparents. I think of them and how they lived with intention, the ways they made a difference. I wonder if I'm doing the same.

My busy schedule flashes before my eyes. Go here. Do that. Commit to this. Say yes to that. My to-do list is never done. My expectations for myself are never met.

I sigh and begin writing on the blank pages in front of me. I explore, tentatively, how I feel God is calling me to a new season—of living entirely differently than before. I squirm in my seat. I question, "God, don't you want me to be busy all the time? Don't you want me to push myself to the limit for you and others? You've been teaching me about relationships. And isn't that what it really means to love?"

It seems my heart hears a whisper in response, "Daughter, I did not come to give you a full life. I came to give you life to the full."

And suddenly everything changes.

I know what it feels like to have a full life that leaves you empty. I don't want to live that way anymore. I imagine you don't either.

When I asked women on *Heart to Heart with Holley* to share their thoughts about this, it quickly became clear that this is a struggle we face in every stage throughout our lives:

> I'm afraid everyone (especially women) in the "modern" world knows this feeling. The problem is I want it all. My boyfriend, my house, my friends, my family, my job . . . and then I feel like I need to do more. . . . Why is it so hard to do the right thing—the best thing? (Marion[1])

> I am a mother of five that works full time as well as having all my children involved in school and sports activities. I feel like I have been running on empty for too long. I pray every day for God's strength to make it through one more day and for him to stay the center of the whirlwind. I know it is only because of him that I can go forward! (Jennifer[2])

> At 76 I still keep on being "busy" and "living life to the full." I need to be reminded sometimes to pause and give thanks for gifts God gives me daily through his grace! (Bernice[3])

God whispers to my heart, *to our hearts*, "I've come to give you better. I've promised you more."

It's a promise. Another dare. And most of all, an invitation.

God's Ultimate Goal

What does God really want for our lives? As we talked about earlier in the book, for many years I would have answered that question this way: "He wants me to be perfect." That belief sent me scrambling after impossible standards, trying to please people, and wearing myself out in the process.

Then Psalm 18 stopped me in my tracks one day. It says, "God's way is perfect ... and he makes my way perfect" (vv. 30, 32 NLT). Did you catch that? *You are not responsible for making yourself perfect.* God will do so—and his idea of perfect is entirely different than ours. In the New Testament, the Greek word for "perfect" is *teleios*, and it's actually more accurately described as maturing growth or completion. For example, an oak tree is the *teleios* of an acorn.[4]

It's also a process that will only be complete in heaven. For now, God will bring our ways into alignment with his. And what are his ways? Love, love, love.

God is love, and *everything* he does is loving. "God is love, and all who live in love live in God, and God lives in them. And as we live in God, our love grows more perfect" (1 John 4:16 NLT). So, again, what does God really want us to do with our lives? Not make them perfect. *Grow in love.*

Love in a biblical sense isn't a touchy-feely, vague experience. It's a verb. It's a series of choices and actions in our lives. So the next step in our process is to look again at your life through the lens of love. How is God asking you to live in love—first with him and then with family, friends, and others he's called you to serve?

Your LIFE

Over the last several chapters we've looked at how God has created you—the strengths he's placed within you, the skills he's developed in you, the way you're wired to connect with others. When we put all of that together, we can capture what he's really calling you to do with your life.

In our culture, that's often called a mission statement. And while I think those can be helpful, it feels like the title can be a bit misleading. As believers, we all ultimately have the same mission. God gave it to us in Galatians 5:6: "The only thing that counts is faith expressing itself through love." We're here to express faith through love—for God, others, and ourselves.

But how that happens does vary with each one of us. By understanding how we're created and called to express love, we find focus and direction. We can say yes to what matters most and no to what isn't necessary without guilt. We can make sure our days are spent wisely and we live well.

So instead of a mission statement, let's talk about your LIFE statement—Love Is Faith Expressed. (Okay, okay, maybe it's a teensy bit cheesy. But it's easy to remember, right? And I am an unashamed acronym fan. So let's just go with it, okay?) I think *express* is such a wonderful word because it implies creativity, individuality, and you doing what you do in a way no one else can. Your LIFE is one-of-a-kind. It's a combination of all we've talked about in the previous chapters. *Drum roll, please . . .* We're now ready to summarize all of that in one sentence.

As I said before, we all start with a common foundation from Galatians 5:6:

I am created and called to express my faith through love . . .

Now you'll finish that statement with your unique way of doing so in the world. That part will have this structure:

. . . especially by (verb ending in "ing") + (what) + (who) + (how)

Here's my LIFE statement:

I am created and called to express my faith through love,

especially by bringing hope and encouragement
(what)

to the hearts of women through words.
(who) *(how)*

Another one might be:

I am created and called to express my faith through love,

especially by <u>meeting the practical needs</u> of
(what)

<u>my family, friends, and community</u> <u>through service.</u>
(who)   *(how)*

Try yours here (this is just a start—you can think and pray about it more later):

I am created and called to express my faith through love, especially by

----

(verb ending in "ing") + (what) + (who) + (how)

The sentence structure above is just a suggestion. You can write your LIFE any way that you'd like. It can be shorter, longer, or in an entirely different format. *There is no wrong way to do this.* Here are some phrases *Heart to Heart with Holley* readers used as part of their statements (when we did this we all used the word "bringing" as the verb).

I am created and called to express my faith through love, especially by bringing . . .

- the love and hope of Christ to hurting friends and strangers through spontaneous, God-inspired acts of service. (Valerie)
- leadership and creativity to my sphere of influence by caring for those God places in my care. (Amy)
- connection and covenant friendship to women through the spoken and written word. (Cari)

- comfort to those in any trouble with the comfort I have received from God. (Melissa)
- faithful service to my family by caring for their needs the way Christ wants. (Tammy)

It will take time for you to create a statement that really feels right. Think of this exercise as a rough draft, a beginning point. There's no pressure to get it done right away—or even to do it at all (I can't believe I just said that). This is just a tool. What matters most is thinking and praying more intentionally about how God wants you to express love through your life.

Circumstances and Seasons

I have a pitcher that I love. I've used it to pour lemonade, water, and tea. I've used it at parties, for dinner with my husband, and when family comes to visit at the holidays.

If that pitcher said, "I'm just made to pour iced tea on Saturdays," then it would only partially understand its purpose. That pitcher might feel like a failure if I wanted to use it to serve orange juice on Sunday mornings instead. But I would be happy about it.

God calls us his "vessel." That means we'll display our LIFE in various situations, amounts, and times. The words we write down are meant not to confine us but rather to bring focus and then set us free to be used by God however he chooses.

For example, speaking encouragement to a tired cashier is just as much living out my statement as writing a book that will be read by thousands. What God wants most in our stories is our hearts. After all, it's not about the size of the word but the meaning behind it. Big or small, he can use it all.

You may have seasons in your life when it seems everything you do flows with your LIFE. Other times you may feel your highest goal is just managing to take a shower. God loves you just the same in both of those. He can use you wherever you are and in whatever you're doing.

Yes, it's important to understand who he's made you to be and what he's called you to do, but living in that is a process that will unfold for a lifetime.

Expressions vs. Expectations

Josie writes down her LIFE statement and posts it on the refrigerator. She smiles as she makes the coffee and thinks, "This is going to be so much better!" Then the phone rings and a neighbor who's chronically in crisis needs her attention. She has to get off the call quickly to get the kids to school, which makes her sigh, "Oh, I'm not a good friend!" The phone call makes her late dropping the kids off, and she realizes the cookies for her son's class party are still on the kitchen counter. She mutters, "There goes being a good mom too."

The rest of the day passes in a blur—the meeting doesn't go as hoped, dinner doesn't taste the way everyone would like, the dishes are still in the sink, and she falls asleep next to her husband thinking, "Sorry, sweetheart, I haven't been much of a wife to you today either." The next morning she looks at the LIFE statement on her refrigerator again and shakes her head. How can one simple statement be so complicated to carry out?

We've all felt like Josie at times. We know what God wants us to do, and we even have his power to do it, but it's still hard to consistently say yes to his calling on our lives. That's often because so many other voices (real or imagined) are demanding our attention as well—telling us what "should" be done.

All those voices we hear have one name: *expectations*.

We have expectations *for* ourselves.

We have expectations *from* others.

As I prayed about this section and what God wanted me to share, I asked him to give me his perspective on expectations. The surprising discovery:

- Expectations are laws we place on ourselves and each other.

Yep, laws.

An expectation equals "You must do X or you will be punished in some way."

Oh, the punishment might be subtle—rejection, guilt we lay on our shoulders, a look across the room that lets us know we didn't measure up. No one is going to throw us in jail. But consequences of the heart can seem even more frightening.

Let's take a look at the expectations in our lives. Try listing one in your life here. For example, "I must say yes every time someone at church asks for help or people will think I'm selfish."

I must _____ or this will

happen: _____ .

What's God's answer to those expectations, to those laws we create for ourselves or let others lay down for us? *Grace.*

LIFE is all about that too.

"You are not under the law, but under grace" (Rom. 6:14). We usually think of that verse in the context of Old Testament law. But it applies to the expectations in our lives as well. We are not to be under anything but grace, the love of Christ, and the leading of the Holy Spirit.

Girls, this is *really* good news. We can kick those expectations to the curb.

Your house doesn't have to be spotless.

Your work doesn't have to be flawless.

You don't have to please that finicky member of your family.

You don't have to look like a page out of a magazine.

You're already enough because Jesus is enough in you. You're loved, accepted, set free to live your LIFE to the fullest.

What Does "Much Required" Really Mean?

As I thought about being free from expectations, a bit of panic started to kick in for me. I thought of a comment recently made by someone in my life: "To whom much is given, much will be required. A lot has been given to you, so a lot is expected of you." I remember how I wilted at those words. And yet I knew that phrase came from the Bible. Why did Jesus say that, and what did he really mean?

I turned to Luke 12 and read that phrase in context. It appears in a story about servants and their master. Yes, it did say to whom much is given much would be required . . . *by the master.* A lot of the expectations in my life aren't from my Master. I make them up or take them on from someone else. In that case, I'm not required to meet them. *And neither are you.* As servants, we're not in control of our own lives, and we don't have to take orders from other servants either. Only God has the authority to tell us our duties, what's required of us.

That made me want to dig deeper. What did God require of me? I pulled out my journal again, ready for a long list. But a quick look at my concordance and a trip over to Micah 6:8 stunned me with its simplicity: "The LORD has told you what is good, and this is what he requires of you: to do what is right, to love mercy, and to walk humbly with your God" (NLT).

Period. End of story. No long list of rules. No endless expectations. It's all there in one verse. And it's all about relationships.

Let's take a closer look at those phrases from Micah 6:8:

○ *To do what is right*—This is about practicing self-control, which leads to loving ourselves as well as others the way God intended.

- *To love mercy*—This is about our relationships with others. We are to love them as ourselves.
- *To walk humbly with your God*—This is about our relationship with God. We are to love him above all.

Amazing, isn't it? Yet it's so difficult to really live this way. The challenge is nothing new. The Galatians, those in one of the early churches, struggled with putting themselves back under the law too. The apostle Paul asks them this question: "After starting your Christian lives in the Spirit, why are you now trying to become perfect by your own human effort?" (Gal. 3:3 NLT). It's a question we're called to consider too.

What expectations in our lives are from God—and what have we added as laws he never intended for us to be under?

We did a little practice listing an expectation above. Write that expectation again below. Then next to it write the real source: yourself, others, or God.

Expectation: I feel like I have to...	Source: *(myself, others, God)*

Ask God to continue uncovering the hidden expectations in your heart as well as their sources. Also ask him to set you free from any that aren't truly from him.

You may fear, "But I won't be loving if I don't have those expectations!" But God is love—whatever he directs you to do will be loving to others too. What you may let go of (and this can be hard!) is what you're doing simply to please people. You are not required to please people. You don't have to meet their expectations. You are a servant with *one* master.

Fear vs. Love

One morning as Josie sticks her to-do list for the day next to her LIFE statement on the refrigerator, she notices a committee meeting that doesn't really seem to fit. She wonders, "Could I say no to that and yes to something better instead?" Her stomach begins to twist, and worries run through her mind. "What if everyone gets mad at me? What if quitting means I'm being selfish?" She pauses, sighs, then calls out to her husband, "I'll be home late tonight!"

One of the hardest parts of embracing our LIFE is letting go of some things we do out of fear. Doing so is always difficult because the lies that have been compelling us to do whatever it is will come rushing back in full force. You're likely to hear, "You won't be loved," "You won't be accepted," "You will fail." Hold on to the truth—you are loved, accepted, enough in Christ. Nothing and no one can take that away from you.

Being led by love is the cure to being driven by fear. "Perfect love drives out fear" (1 John 4:18).

If you're not sure whether you're motivated by fear or love in a certain activity, you can try writing it out this way:

◦ I feel compelled to

(Example: Have a completely clean house)

◦ This is motivated by . . .

Fear	Love
(what people will think of me)	*(desiring to make a haven for my family)*

As you grow in love, you'll move further away from fear and toward love in different areas of your life. You don't have to make that happen right now. Instead, just be aware of it and begin asking

God to help you change. "He who began a good work in you will carry it on to completion" (Phil. 1:6).

When you think of what you might want to say no to in your life, the things that are all the way on the fear side would be the first to consider. Fear can creep in at times even when we're doing exactly what God wants us to do in love. But if the only reason we're doing something is out of fear, then it's not from God. As we talked about before, "God gave us a spirit not of fear but of power and love and self-control" (2 Tim. 1:7 ESV).

Pause for a moment and consider: If you knew you would be completely loved and accepted no matter what, then which items would be crossed off your to-do list for good? Consider letting go of those things in your life. If it's something that you really need to do, then begin asking God to heal your heart so that you can do so more out of love and less out of fear.

At one point in my life, it seemed God kept emptying my hands of so much. I asked, "Why are you doing that?" And I slowly came to realize God has to empty us of ourselves before he can fill us with him. Does that mean we have to let go of all he's given? No, but we hold it loosely. We surrender. We say, "Not my will but yours be done."

And we look at our lives closely, like one mining for gold. We are of great worth, amazing women of God, and that means what we allow into our lives should be of value too. We can sift through our schedules and ask, "Does that really belong there? Is this a glimmer of false security? Is fear compelling me to do this?" We filter, sort, pay close attention. We toss away what is not of him and deeply treasure all that remains. Then we hold it up to the light and polish it until it shines even more brightly—and we do too.

As you let go of some things you're doing out of fear, it may seem as if a void opens up in your life. Our expectations are often also our *motivations*. If the expectations are gone, then why do you do what you do? It's not about being free to do whatever you want (which you may fear might happen if you don't have those requirements). The goal is to replace those expectations (the law) with the same thing Jesus did and what we've talked about all along—love.

Just Say No to Guilt

The closer you get to what God has truly called you to do in your LIFE journey, the more the enemy will resist you. You'll likely have thoughts like, "Oh, I've totally messed this up," or "I don't do this enough," or "How can I live this out when I am a stay-at-home mom/have to work/am battling chronic illness right now?"

Listen, girl, if it's important enough for you to put in your LIFE statement, then I can almost guarantee you are already living it out in some way. For example, maybe creativity is part of your statement and you long to be an artist with paintings in a gallery, but right now you're raising toddlers. Then I bet you're finger painting with them, or teaching them colors, or helping them find beauty in the world.

Whatever you are wired by God to do, you'll find a way to do where you are—and *all* of that is equally important to him. We tend to think there's a pinnacle to our purpose, a high point we have to reach. But God cares more about the journey and our partnership with him in the process. Remember what we talked about earlier? Perfection is simply about growth, a little at a time.

When You Worry, You've Wasted Your Life

We sit and talk. Eventually she clears her throat and quietly asks, "What do you do if you feel like you've wasted your life?" The silence hangs thick in the air between us.

It's a heavy question of the heart.

And I think of the One who had the most meaningful existence ever. For so many years, he was simply a carpenter.

I say this out loud, pondering.

"He didn't need more practice," I say, "and it sure seems like he could have started his ministry earlier and gotten more done. But for some inexplicable reason, he spent years working with wood. Years we would have called wasted."

She looks up, smiles. We part ways. Next time I see her, she holds a sheet of paper in her hand. It has these words on it. I ask her if I can share them with you. She says yes.

> Why did he need to be a carpenter? Maybe, just maybe, he was a carpenter for me. . . . Each hurt is a board, each disappointment a piece of wood, and each trial a plank.
>
> Jesus, the carpenter, is taking each piece of wood and nailing it together. He is nailing together a future that is unclear to me, but I have peace because he is my carpenter. I take great comfort in Ephesians 2:10: "For we are God's workmanship, created in Christ Jesus to do good works, which God prepared in advance for us to do" [NIV 1984].
>
> I understand that my past was not wasted. He is using it all to "build" me so I can do the good works God has prepared for me to do. I don't know what he has in store for me in the next phase of my life; however, it doesn't matter because he is building me into his masterpiece.

Those "wasted" years? In the carpenter's hands they can be transformed into a beautiful part of your purpose.

We might think that Jesus could have gotten a lot more accomplished if God had just let him get started sooner. But God isn't interested in how much we can do. If he can create the world in seven days with a few words, then getting it done isn't an issue for him! Instead God is interested in us doing only what he's asked us to do, when he wants us to do it, and most of all simply living in love along the way.

Keep Growing, Girl

You are *free*. Free to love. Free to live in joy. Free to be who you are. If you're loving God, others, and yourself, then *you're already doing enough*. That's right. And you're already amazing because you are God's creation, his child, and he lives in you. Sounds scandalous, doesn't it? But it's true.

What God wants most of all is you. Just as you are. Then he'll show you how he wants to use your life to partner with him in fulfilling his purposes. It won't be a burden but instead a glorious adventure—with plenty of room for mistakes, growth, and joy along the way. Bonnie Gray from the blog *Faith Barista* beautifully says it this way:

> It encourages me to know that Jesus knows how unnatural it is for me to come to Him as I am. I know that the Holy Spirit prays for me during these moments because out of nowhere, I'll be struck with how much God loves me, and how much I need Him.
>
> And I go to Him. Not because I'm so great in any sense. But because God is great in His love for me.[5]

I'm looking at the trees in my backyard as I write these words. I can't see them growing. But I know it's happening because day after day, year after year, they simply keep reaching a little higher toward heaven. I imagine for a moment that each leaf is a little bit of love. And I think of you—how you're out there growing too. Day after day, year after year, simply reaching a little higher toward heaven, drawing closer to God's heart.

That's all he wants, sweet friend. Not your striving. Not your standards. Just you.

The trees stretch out their arms, and we stretch out our hearts. I close my eyes and imagine the arms of the One who loves us reaching back, always finding us, always willing to carry us, always reminding us that life is about love—giving it, receiving it, gloriously growing until our hearts are home.

9

What Are **My Next Steps?**

Here's how my morning went. I got up early (which is a minor miracle), ate breakfast with my husband, rode the exercise bike for twenty minutes while reading my Bible, took a shower, and sat down to pray and write in my journal about this chapter.

Then I checked my email.

One hour, fifty-four messages, six websites, and two Facebook stops later, I felt like the world was falling apart. I had more items on my task list than time in my day, unanswered requests, and a morning that seemed like it had quickly gotten derailed.

So what did I do? Exactly what every deeply spiritual woman does in these cases.

I ate a chocolate brownie with peanut butter frosting.

At 9:00 a.m.

Then I laughed long and hard at myself because this chapter is supposed to be about implementing your Life Is Faith Expressed statement effectively. And a big part of that is being organized, right? Ha ha ha. Pass the brownies, honey.

I will be the first to admit that I don't have this part figured out when it comes to schedules, detailed lists, and a fully organized world.

And I'm starting to believe (warning: scandalous statement coming) that it doesn't matter much to God. Did I just say that? It must be the peanut butter frosting talking.

What I mean is that we put a lot of pressure on ourselves to do things a certain way and/or to do it all. But God doesn't put those standards on us. Remember how we talked in the last chapter about expectations being like living under the law? Well, the woman-made standards in our lives are the same way.

Are we to be responsible stewards of our lives, time, emotions, energy, and resources? Yes, of course. But how that looks in our daily lives is going to be as unique as we are. You have a purpose no one else has, and how that unfolds will look different for you than for any other woman in your life.

Run YOUR Race

LIFE gives us direction, but we still need to know specifically what steps to take next. These verses show us the starting line: "Let us throw off everything that hinders and the sin that so easily entangles. And let us run with perseverance the race marked out for us, fixing our eyes on Jesus, the pioneer and perfecter of faith" (Heb. 12:1–2).

What Hinders You?

First we're to look in our lives for *what hinders*. That's anything in your life that is getting in the way of you living God's purpose.

Rebecca likes to do things herself. It feels like helping others (after all, they're busy too), and it also ensures that things turn out the way she wants. But Rebecca's plate just keeps getting fuller. She knows God wants her to spend more time with the college girls at her church. Unlike many of the other responsibilities in her life, that one brings her joy and fills her up. She also sees a real difference in the lives of the girls. But right now it seems to land at the bottom of her list. Rebecca drifts off to sleep, exhausted, thinking, "Maybe someday when things slow down . . ."

Rebecca's long to-do list is something that hinders. To throw it off and run her race, she's probably going to need to learn to delegate some tasks and let go of others. As you can probably tell, something that "hinders" is anything that trips you up and slows you down. This can be hard to recognize because unlike "sin that entangles," what hinders us often seems good. And many times it is—it's just not what's best. My wise college mentor, Beth English, used to say, "Holley, the hardest choices in life aren't between good and bad. They're between good and best."

Wayne Cordeiro, author of *Leading on Empty*, says 85 percent of what we do, anyone can do. For example, watching television, checking email, and attending meetings. Another 10 percent could be done by someone if we trained them. That last 5 percent is what only we can do. After facing burnout, making new choices about that 5 percent became a life-changing revelation for Wayne:

> I had to rethink what was most important to me—what God had asked me to do—and how I would restructure my life. I had to think what my last 5 percent would include. What were the things that only I could do and, if neglected, would affect the rest of my life? Here are the responsibilities I wrote down:
>
> 1. A vibrant, growing relationship with my Lord and Savior, Jesus Christ
> 2. A healthy and genuine relationship with my spouse
> 3. An authentic family that is close to God and close to one another
> 4. A God-pleasing ministry

5. A physically healthy body and a creative soul
6. Taking time to enjoy life with family and friends

Wayne goes on to say, "Your choice of what is most important will shape your soul. We won't be accountable for how much we have done, but for how much we have done of what *he asked us to do*."[1]

You have a gift to offer the world, a calling only you can fulfill, a race only you can run. Throw off everything that hinders and move forward in all God has for you.

What Entangles You?

Next we're looking for *sin that entangles*.

Rebecca sometimes turns to gossip or criticism to vent. "She's so lazy," Rebecca tells her husband. "If she had any motivation at all, I wouldn't have to do everything myself." She pours out more of her frustration but ends up feeling even worse. And nothing in the situation changes, so she repeats the same cycle the next day.

Like all of us, Rebecca sometimes spends time and emotional energy with little return. Sin can momentarily make us feel better, but in the end it's a high price to pay. It quickly empties our emotional bank accounts and separates us from God and others.

When we find ourselves entangled in sin, we can ask forgiveness, turn away from the sin, and get back on the path to keep going in our race. This battle with sin isn't a one-time fix. As the apostle Paul tells us, it's a step-by-step reliance on Christ:

> Now if I do what I do not want to do, it is no longer I who do it, but it is sin living in me that does it. So I find this law at work: When I want to do good, evil is right there with me. For in my inner being I delight in God's law; but I see another law at work in me, waging war against the law of my mind and making me a prisoner of the law of sin at work within me. What a wretched man I am! Who will rescue me from this body that is subject to death? Thanks

be to God, who delivers me through Jesus Christ our Lord!
So then, I myself in my mind am a slave to God's law, but
in my sinful nature a slave to the law of sin. (Rom. 7:20–25)

Dare to embrace who you are. Dare to do those weird things
you do. Dare to trust God's whispers into your life more than the
demands of the world around you about "the right way." You have
the Holy Spirit within you, and he will show you what you need to
change in a way that's gentle, life giving, and affirming.

Let's revisit the two areas we talked about above: what hinders and
sin that entangles. Pause for a few moments here to pray and think
through what those might be for you. Then jot them down below:

- My LIFE statement (rewrite it here):

_____

- What hinders me (anything that holds me back):

_____

_____

- Sin that entangles me (anything that trips me up):

_____

_____

Let's move forward. With sin, the process begins by acknowledging that we've hurt God. We ask forgiveness, receive it, and
then request his help in starting to live differently. Sometimes the
process of change is instant and complete. Other times, it takes
place over a period of time as we learn new patterns of behavior
to replace what we've been doing.

With what isn't sinful but simply hinders us, it's also a matter of
growth over time. Remember the true biblical definition of perfection? It's about maturity and becoming complete. That takes time
and many small steps in the right direction.

Move Forward in Faith

Everything that hinders.

Sin that so easily tangles.

Those are the obstacles God wants us to clear out of our paths. You can stop worrying about everything else.

Read that again, girl.

You can stop worrying about everything else.

Yes, that includes how clean your neighbor thinks your house should be, that "suggestion" the preacher gave so adamantly from the pulpit about what you have to do, the better way your friend seems to handle that part of her life. *All of it.*

We are running "the race marked out *for us*" (Heb. 12:1). That means we're only concerned about the obstacles *in our lane.* If someone feels she needs to do something, then let her do it—it's probably in her lane. But that doesn't mean it's in yours.

This isn't about self-improvement. It's about aligning our lives with love in the way God created us to do. To do that, we need a lot of grace and an approach that makes sense based on who God made us. Every runner has a rhythm that works best for her. You're the same way. When we set out to make changes, we need to be sure we're moving to be more of who God made us—not more like someone else.

I remember sitting with a group of artists during a brainstorming session one day. We looked through magazines to get ideas and inspiration. I found a feature that shared different rooms where creative people worked. One overflowed with supplies, swatches of fabric, and collected items. I remarked to the girl sitting next to me, "I could never write in a space like that. I need my house to be uncluttered before I can create." She replied, "That's because you need to shut out everything else and focus internally to write. As an artist, I need to be surrounded by things that I can see when I look up because that's what gives me new ideas as I go."

She was completely right. For years, I'd felt guilty about not having a home filled with more decorative items. I felt like a failure and as if I couldn't possibly be truly creative. My artist friend had probably carried around guilt about not having a home that was a bit tidier and more orderly. But we both had what we needed to do what we were called to do.

It's the same way with every area of our lives. Any changes we make need to support who we are and the way we're intended to love others. We need to pray for wisdom and then trust the part of us that says, "This works for you." Like me, we may not even be able to articulate why until someone else points it out to us. We can waste a lot of energy trying to fix what isn't broken.

What Are Your Next Steps?

When my husband and I vacation, we walk everywhere. There's a moment when I panic a little—usually when my husband pulls out the map and cheerfully says, "Let's go here, here, and here." And I reply, "That's a looonnnggg way. Can't we just go to Starbucks?"

But we set out . . . and by the end of the day we've made it and I'm happy. I've learned the trick is not giving in to that moment when the journey seems like too much.

Just start with one step.

Now that the path is clear for you to run your race, you can start thinking about what God is actually asking you to do with your LIFE. That statement is intended to be general, but when it comes to our everyday lives, we need to get more specific.

When we start taking several steps in a particular direction, it becomes a destination (in other words, a goal). Where we're heading should always be led by Jesus and in line with our LIFE. The idea of doing more than just taking some small steps can be intimidating. But when it comes to making changes in our lives,

I'm starting to realize that the process doesn't have to be as complicated as we often make it.

I've got plenty of experience setting unrealistic goals. Around the new year I start imagining how I will exercise for an hour every morning, bond with my husband every night, and write the most brilliant book ever published.

However, three days into the plan, I realize my shiny new ambitions will never be realized. And while all of my good intentions are staring me in the face, I realize something is drastically wrong. Rather than providing much-needed motivation, the goals created to help me live a full, balanced life have instead become the seeds of future disappointment.

One day I was driving to work and telling myself once again, "When things slow down, I will go to the gym and work out all the time. I'll get in shape. It will be great." Then I thought, "I've been telling myself this for five years. Things are never going to slow down. I've got to do what I can." That was the beginning of a revolution.

The "Do What You Can Plan"

The "Do What You Can Plan" is exactly what it sounds like—you do what you can to take steps and move in the direction God has for your LIFE. It began as an article I wrote for an online magazine called *Zia*. The magazine is no longer in existence, but the principles I wrote about are still very much a part of my life.

For me, the "Do What You Can Plan" meant doing whatever little bit I could each day. For example, if I could only fit in ten sit-ups, then that's all I would do. A year later, I'd lost the weight I wanted to shed and dropped a clothing size. I was shocked that I'd actually reached my goal by doing so little. So I decided to start applying the "Do What You Can Plan" to other areas of my life and spent some time figuring out exactly what made it work. Here are a few things I discovered along the way.

∼ *Small Can Be Really Big* ∼

We often get caught up in thinking we have to do something really big to achieve our goals, but sometimes the little things really can make a difference. Someone once told me that coming to the point where change happens is like adding one drop of water to a bucket every day. One day the bucket just overflows, but it's all the little drops along the way that made it happen. So when you're setting goals and thinking about the steps to reach them, think small. Say tomorrow you make a personal goal to walk a mile every day. If you take your dog for a walk around the block and that's all you can do for the day—that's great. Over time, those steps will add up, and you'll go farther than you imagined.

Jesus said if we have faith as a mustard seed, then we can move mountains. Have you seen a mustard seed? I was shocked the first time I did! Those things are *tiny*. It seems the point isn't how much we have on our own but whose hands we place it in. God knows how to turn our little bit into a whole lot.

∼ *Easy Is Not a Four-Letter Word* ∼

We all lead busy lives. Figuring out how to reach our goals when so many other things are asking for our attention is tough. I confess that I love to make complicated goals that are hard to maintain. The perfectionist in me comes out in full force, and before I know it, my goals need three notebooks and four spreadsheets just to keep track of them.

But the easy way is often the best way. For example, if you are trying to get in shape, think about how you can do that as part of your everyday routine. I do squats when I dry my hair in the morning and while unloading laundry. My husband thinks this is hilarious, and the dog shoots me a look of confusion now and then, but it's a small price to pay. Asking yourself how a goal can fit your everyday life is more than easy; it's essential.

God does ask us to do really hard things sometimes. When that's the case, we need to obey. But it seems we often use our energy and emotion on things that don't matter as much. Then when he does give us a big assignment, we're already exhausted. This is about using what we've got in the most effective way so we can be ready for whatever is ahead in God's plans for us!

~ *The Meaning Matters* ~

If your goal is a good one, it will take more than killer willpower to see you through. For me, a goal needs to have deeper meaning. If all I want to do is fit into a smaller pair of jeans, that's not enough to motivate me. I want to be fit so that I can have the energy and motivation to love God and those around me. When I don't feel good physically, I'm not a very fun person to be around. I growl, eat way too much chocolate, and in general don't make the world a nicer place to be. Dr. Gary Oliver, executive director of the Center for Relationship Enrichment, says that focusing on growth rather than change can give goals more meaning. How does this goal fit with your LIFE? Change is outward while growth is inward. By figuring out how your goal fits with something deep inside you, you will be much more motivated to do what you can to accomplish it. "Seek first his kingdom and his righteousness, and all these things will be given to you as well" (Matt. 6:33).

~ *What to Do with Slipups and Setbacks* ~

The seemingly evil twins of slipups and setbacks always seem to get the best of me when setting goals. I have good intentions, but before I know it, I'm downing the last piece of cheesecake at a party. The "Do What You Can Plan" has two little words to say about slipups and setbacks: "Oh, well." If it's actually a sin (such as using food to satisfy a need that only God can), then we need three words: "Please forgive me."

Since this plan is about doing what you can, not achieving perfection, what matters most is just getting up and doing what you can tomorrow. Slipups and setbacks are also great opportunities for learning. Think about what you might do differently in the future. Even create a strategy if needed. For example, you could eat a healthy dinner before you go to the next party so you're not ravenously hungry.

God gave us grace for a reason—he knew we'd need it. And he promises an endless supply. What matters most to him isn't that you always get it right but instead that you stay right by his side.

~ *Sunny Side Up* ~

The "Do What You Can Plan" is all about keeping things positive. It's a lot friendlier than the "You Tried Again This Year but Failed as Usual Plan." Our brains are wired to respond better to being told what we can do than what we can't. If you've ever tried giving up chocolate for a week and found yourself shrieking like a banshee by Wednesday, you know what I mean. Rather than figuring out what you're not going to do, think about what you are going to do instead. For example, next time I throw chocolate to the wind, I'll splurge on strawberries and pineapple to take its place when I have a craving for something sweet.

Another part of staying sunny is celebrating. I'm trying to get better at savoring accomplishments. I tend to reach a goal and then instantly set out toward a new one. Celebrating can look different for everyone. Maybe you go out to eat at your favorite restaurant, buy some new shoes, take a nap—or all of the above. Celebrating is positive reinforcement, a concept we're all familiar with. It makes our brains more willing to cooperate next time we set a goal.

Gratitude is also at the heart of celebration. Sometimes we're so busy pushing forward that we forget to stop and thank God for how far he's taken us. God is there for us in hard times, and he loves rejoicing with us too. So let him share the joy.

Going the Distance

The "Do What You Can Plan" is essentially about making goals work for you rather than the other way around. It's about small changes that make a big difference. It's about knowing that life is a meaningful journey and every step takes us closer to where we want to go. And along the way, it's okay to eat chocolate sometimes, to mess up, and to make things a little easier if we can. We can all do a lot if we just do a little. And with God, there's nothing that's impossible for us. Here's even more good news:

- Yes, Jesus says we can do all things through him—
- but he never says we have to do it all!

Deidra Riggs, who blogs at *Jumping Tandem*, wrote a post on the website (in)courage about going to the gym and telling the trainer she wanted to run a half-marathon. The trainer inquired about Deidra's running history and gently suggested a 5k might be a great place to start. Then she helped Deidra make a plan to do it. The next day Deidra stepped on the treadmill feeling a bit disappointed, until wisdom from her trainer changed everything:

> "Distance first. Then speed," she said. And with those two short sentences, I think she just may have saved me from disaster.
>
> Because we big picture people want it all and we want it now, don't we? We don't always consider the many steps it takes to reach a goal....
>
> I probably would have cranked up the speed on that treadmill to some ridiculous number, worn myself out in two minutes flat, and given up on the whole idea. But those two sentences rang in my head for the entire twenty minutes it took me to run my little 1.5 miles.
>
> I was pleased with myself. Motivated, even. And in that moment I realized that I wasn't ready for the "all"

that we big picture people crave. Not yet. I needed this one little piece, first. This accomplishment. This is what I could handle right then. This is what fit. This was something I could build on.[2]

Maybe, like Deidra, you're ready to run a marathon in life. Or you might be sitting on the curb wondering if you even have what it takes to make it to the end of the block. Either way, the best place to start is with one small step. It's the only way to bigger things with God. As Jesus said, "Whoever can be trusted with very little can also be trusted with much" (Luke 16:10).

∼ My "Do What You Can Plan" ∼

Change God wants me to make:	Small next step:	How I'll celebrate:

Your Organizational Personality

As you set out to make changes, let's get a bit more clarity about how you approach life. This is important because the thing about change is that it takes time. And that requires structure and discipline. That's what trips a lot of us up. We pick the right change but the wrong way (for us) to go about getting it accomplished.

So let's look at some typical ways women approach life. Then circle the one that sounds most like you.

The Princess of Planning

You love order and structure. It gives you great satisfaction to take your thoughts and put them in tangible form—whether that is in a planner, a digital calendar, or a list. You want to know what's coming and be prepared. You enjoy details and can relax most when you know everything is in order. You like to think ahead and usually make time to do so. Others value your responsibility, conscientiousness, and consistency.

- *Strengths:* You get things done. You don't overlook details because you have them all recorded. You plan effectively and usually accomplish your goals.
- *Next steps for your "Do What You Can Plan":* Set aside time to create a concrete strategy for change. Write out what you want to accomplish and the steps to making it happen. Purchase or create whatever supplies you need to do so—a calendar, new journal, or chart—and put time in your schedule to pray and review your progress.
- *Watch out for:* Your goals becoming more important than your relationships with God and other people, being too hard on yourself, and becoming impatient when you don't see measurable results quickly.

The Queen of Creativity

You like variety and thrive on what's new. You have good intentions when you begin but often get bored with your goals before they're completed. You don't necessarily like details or feel compelled to keep track of your life in a tangible way. You like your options open. Too much order or planning feels restrictive. You're inspired by ideas, the intangible, beauty, and learning. You tackle a challenge for the joy of it, and when it's not as much fun, it may be hard to continue. But if you're deeply passionate you can work long and hard and create in a way that's often amazing to others. You put your heart into your daily life and operate on intuition much of the time. You may not be able to articulate exactly how something will get done, but you're definitely clear on why it matters and who it will benefit.

- *Strengths:* Your creativity brings freshness and excitement to the world. Others enjoy you because you encourage and inspire them to see things in new ways.
- *Next steps for your "Do What You Can Plan":* Get rid of the idea that you will find the perfect system and stay with it forever. Embrace your creativity when it comes to pursuing your goals. Remove structure except where it's absolutely necessary. Buy an unlined journal, put a whiteboard on the refrigerator, start a notebook of ideas. Add variety to your plans so that your goal stays the same but how you achieve it can change multiple times throughout the process.
- *Watch out for:* Chasing after the new so much that you abandon worthy goals prematurely, giving in to boredom and quitting rather than finding a creative solution to push through it, and rebelling against all structure and order.

The Royal Highness of Relationships

You believe life is all about connecting with others. You focus on who is in front of you, who's on the phone, or that email you just got that needs a response. Your schedule revolves around people, not projects. The only purpose for planning or tasks would be so that you can build your relationships even more. Your warmth and friendliness ensure your social life is full. When someone needs you, you drop everything to make sure you can be there for them. The direction of your life is determined by those around you.

- *Strengths:* You make people feel valued, loved, and important. You are friendly, open, and there whenever anyone needs a hand or just a hug.

○ *Next steps for your "Do What You Can Plan":* Because you're so responsive to the needs of others, you may overlook your own. Begin to look at goals you might see as selfish (e.g., exercising) as an extension of the way you care for others (e.g., it gives you energy to play with your kids). You're not going to be motivated to do something unless you find a way it helps someone else too. So intentionally list that out with your goals and remember it. Also, whenever possible include others in accomplishing your goals by either having them join you in what you're doing or keeping you accountable.

○ *Watch out for:* Abandoning your goals because they are different from the goals of others, listening to what people want you to do before you take time to ask God what he wants, and allowing others to put unrealistic demands on you that make it difficult to take care of yourself.

These are just intended to be a lighthearted look at how we can approach change. You may see yourself a little bit in each one—or you might make up your own! The point is just to acknowledge that even if we have the same changes in mind as someone else, how we make those happen will be different. Who God made you is good, so go with it, girl.

Trying to force yourself to live in a way that doesn't make sense for who you are will just lead to frustration and wasted energy. It's okay to figure out what works best for you, and who knows, it might even be *fun*. As long as it's in line with God's Word, feel free to move ahead. "I run in the path of your commands, for you have set my heart free" (Ps. 119:32 NIV 1984).

Keep Realigning Your Life with Love

As you begin to do what you can and live in grace, love will begin to grow even more in your life. With each choice you make, you become a little more of who God made you and draw a little closer to his purpose for your life. The LIFE that's yours to share with others becomes clearer. It's like the lines in the road keeping you on course.

Go out there and run the race he's got for you, girl. The world is watching and heaven is cheering you on (and I am too).

10

Is It Okay to Take Care of **Myself?**

Jamie leans into the wall and places her head in her hands. "I'm so tired of being tired," she whispers. She thinks about asking for help, taking time away, just doing things differently. But another voice seems to interrupt, "Just get a grip and do what you need to do. A lot of people are counting on you. What's the matter with you?" She's heard those thoughts before. Jamie looks up and sighs, then tells herself she's just got to make it through another day.

Women are a generous gender. We give to our spouses, kids, neighbors, co-workers, church members, friends, and even the grocery clerk who is having a bad day. We pour out until one day we wonder, "Why do I feel so empty?"

One reason is a myth that says, "It's selfish to take care of myself." Oh, most of us would check "false" on that one if we had a test in front of us. But when we look at how we live, the answer seems quite different. We just talked about running your own race, and every athlete knows that self-care is essential to crossing the finish line well. In much the same way, taking care of yourself is going to be important to accomplishing your "Do What You Can Plan," fulfilling God's purpose for your life, and loving the people in your life well.

Another way to think of it is like a bank account for your heart. Certain things are like deposits: coffee with a friend, a long bubble bath, time spent praying. Others are withdrawals: an overwhelming project at work, a child with the flu, an especially busy season of life. We live in a fallen world, and there's never going to be a time when our emotional bank account always stays full. We don't need to feel guilty about it getting low sometimes. But we do need to be intentional about replenishing it so that we have something to give next time we're needed.

These are three common ways people try to refill their emotional energy accounts:

- Trying to earn the approval of others—In this mindset, we treat life like a job and the approval of others like a paycheck.

- Taking what we want because we're entitled to it—In this scenario, we grab all we can get because we believe we deserve it.

- Receiving what our hearts need as a gift of grace—We remember Jesus said to love others *as ourselves* (see Matt. 22:39), so we invest in ourselves because he says we're of great value.

I've done all of the above. You too? Our goal is to move more toward the third option. So let's pause for a moment and take a look at your emotional energy account.

Withdrawals	Deposits
(things that take emotional energy in my life right now)	*(things that increase/restore my emotional energy in my life right now)*
Example: Conflict with my teenage daughter	*Example: Coffee with a dear friend*

Hint: If you're having trouble thinking of things, then fill in the blanks below:

○ I feel the most drained after I

_____

(withdrawals)

○ I feel the most energized after I

_____

(deposits)

Sometimes we overestimate the emotional balance in our account because the withdrawals may be *good* things. For example, a teacher who is an introvert may love the kids in her classroom and feel very called to the profession. But being with other people all day long is going to be a withdrawal. Does that mean she should stop teaching? Nope, not at all. It just means she's going to need some things in the "Deposit" column so she can be restored.

As women, we often sabotage ourselves with false guilt. We tell ourselves that being married is a privilege, having children is a joy, going to work each day is a blessing—so we just need to suck it up and stop being so tired all the time. We should put on a happy face, say thanks, and get on with it, right?

As we've talked about before, how you feel is legitimate. What takes away from your emotional energy as well as what adds to it isn't bad or good. It's neutral. It's just reality. It usually doesn't say anything about what kind of person you are, how much you love the people in your life, or how much faith you have. It's just part of the way you're made.

When you give to a charity or another organization, it's a good choice. But it's still a withdrawal from your bank account. If you endlessly gave without replacing those funds, you'd end up bankrupt. You wouldn't be able to give to the charity any longer or cover the needs in your life. That's a lot like how our hearts work too. Even Jesus took time away to be renewed. It's not selfish to make a deposit in your emotional bank account. It's an investment that you'll be able to use to bless someone later.

Some withdrawals in our lives do need to be stopped. Imagine if you gambled away your life savings. Addictions, affairs, and other issues make us a slave to sin and drain away everything we have. If you're stuck in a destructive pattern, find someone you trust who can help you get free before you're emotionally and spiritually spent.

You are the only one who knows what's in your emotional bank account. "Each heart knows its own bitterness, and no one else can share its joy" (Prov. 14:10). So it's your responsibility to understand how God has made you and what you need.

We've talked about this before and it's worth mentioning again: women tend to compare. My friend who's an uber-extrovert gets a huge deposit in her emotional account every time she goes to a conference. I, on the other hand, go home with few funds left even though I love being there. So I know that after I get home, I need time alone to refuel and be ready to go again.

I don't believe in balance—there's never a time in our lives when the withdrawals and deposits work out perfectly. Life is too messy and unpredictable. That's not the goal. Instead, it's simply to be aware of what we need and give ourselves permission to receive it.

No matter what renews us, the source is ultimately the same: "Come to me, all you who are weary and burdened, and I will give you rest" (Matt. 11:28). Jesus doesn't want us to be exhausted. He doesn't expect us to be all things to all people. So take a deep breath, lean back into his love, and ask him what your heart needs to be filled with today.

Why It's So Hard to Receive

We feel the exhaustion. We know when we're discouraged. We sense the loneliness. So why is it so hard to receive what we need?

Receiving Is Risky

Jamie desperately wants to ask for help on a project at work. But she's afraid if she does, it won't seem as if she adds as much value to the team. So she stays late again and finishes everything herself. "Surely they wouldn't ever doubt my worth now," she tells herself as she finally closes her eyes to sleep.

In order to receive, we have to open our hearts, hands, and lives. We put ourselves in a position that's vulnerable. When we give, we're usually more in control. We get to determine what, how, and when. It's a risk—but it's usually one we've calculated. Receiving feels messy, more unpredictable. But it's essential. Look at the world around you. Everything in nature is about give and take, offering and receiving, grasping and releasing. If you only feel safe when you're giving and consistently resist receiving, then you may have some fears holding you back from getting what you need.

Try: writing down or saying out loud to someone you trust what you're actually afraid will happen if you receive.

Receiving Feels Selfish

Jamie's husband stands beside her at the kitchen sink. "Hey, why don't you let me finish those dishes? You look exhausted." Jamie looks up at him quizzically. She knows he doesn't like doing dishes. She would love to take him up on the offer, but then she thinks, "It's not fair to make him do this just because I'm tired. I need to do my part." "Thanks," she responds, "but I can take care of it." Her husband sighs and walks away. A few minutes later she hears the TV turn on in the living room. Jamie dries the last plate and wonders why she's feeling resentful.

We touched on this before, and it's probably the most common reason women avoid receiving. We've got big, generous hearts and we want to bless those around us. We long to be good wives, mothers, and friends. When we receive, it feels like we're taking away from someone else. After all, "it is more blessed to give than to receive" (Acts 20:35), right? But in the upside-down kingdom of God, what looks like taking is actually giving. You bless others by letting them give to you—just like you feel blessed when you give to them. If you're always receiving and never willing to give, then you may have some entitlement to hand over to God. But I imagine very few of you are that way. For most women, we're more likely to be out of balance by giving far more than we allow ourselves to receive.

Try: saying yes when someone offers to help you.

Receiving Seems Unproductive

The kids are in bed. The house has been picked up. Jamie settles down on the couch and opens a novel. But before she's through the first chapter, a thousand thoughts seem to run through her mind. "I could be cleaning out that closet. I probably should get a jump start on that report for work. What was that last item on my to-do list?" She sets the book down and grabs her list from the counter. By midnight she has several more items checked off, but the next morning she wakes up feeling even more behind.

We like our to-do lists and all those check marks at the end of the day. It's hard to add something like "read a book" or "enjoy a walk with a friend" to our list of highly urgent tasks. Often when we spend time receiving we walk away feeling guilty and as if we're wasting our time. But receiving is actually an investment in our future productivity.

I hate stopping to put gas in my tank. I'm usually zipping from one place to another. Pulling over feels like a hassle. If I decide to skip that stop, I might make it a few more miles down the road faster, but eventually it's going to catch up with me. Filling your gas tank after you've made it all the way to empty is a lot more trouble than practicing a little prevention. Just like our cars, we've got warning lights. It might be exhaustion, irritability, anxiety, or depression. When one of those starts creeping in, just look at it as the little light on your internal dashboard telling you, "Stop for a refill soon!" Over a lifetime, you'll actually be a lot more productive if you learn to receive.

Try: treating receiving just like any other task on your list.

Receiving Feels Undeserved

Jamie's little girl runs up to her. "Mommy, you're so wonderful!" she declares. Startled by this sudden expression of affection, Jamie brushes her daughter's hands away before she even realizes what she's doing. After all, she hasn't been the mom she'd like to be this week. Her daughter looks confused. "I'm sorry, honey. Mommy didn't mean to do that. Come here and let me try again."

Sometimes we push others away or withhold what we need from ourselves because we don't believe we've earned it. When we're better, skinnier, wealthier, holier, or a better mom, wife, or friend, then we'll deserve to receive. We treat receiving as a reward. But God clearly tells us that receiving is always about grace. That's true for the spiritual aspect of our lives and every other area too. If we wait until we're perfect to receive, then it's never going to happen. You can receive now because you are God's child, dearly loved, redeemed, chosen, and cherished. You can receive not because of what you do but because of who you are in him.

Try: resisting the urge to deny compliments or push away affection from others. Simply say, "Thank you."

Receiving Simply Isn't Part of Our Plan

Jamie stands in front of the refrigerator and marks another event on the family calendar. Then she checks her email and accepts a meeting request for the following week. Her phone buzzes with a reminder about a birthday party starting in a few hours. Jamie laughs and sighs to herself as she thinks about her schedule. "It seems like everyone gets a place in my plans but me."

Receiving seems like it would just happen naturally, right? But life is often too busy or complicated for that to happen. Think back to your "Do What You Can Plan." Did you put anything about receiving in there? If not, then you're missing an important piece. Life is busy. Phones ring. Emails arrive. Guests show up. We think, "When things settle down, then I'll take better care of myself." But things never do settle down. There's no such thing as normal. There will always be more to do, ways to improve, and new items on your list to accomplish. Receiving requires making it a priority and part of your plan just like you would anything else that matters in life.

Try: including receiving along with the other plans you make.

Receive, Then Invest

Albert Lexie has been shining shoes for over forty years. In 1981, he created the goal of donating $100,000 in tips to help a children's hospital. Little by little, Albert made it happen. It wasn't all at once—instead it came through a series of small deposits which he intentionally made knowing that those would all add up to a lot.

Whenever we're talking about receiving, it helps to remember what we want to invest in with our LIFE. It's all about paying it forward.

Most of us are familiar with the parable of the talents Jesus tells in Matthew 25, but let's do a quick recap. A master goes on a journey and entrusts three servants with talents (a talent was a certain amount of money in those days). The first two servants invest what they've been given. The master praises them when he returns. The third servant buries his talent, and the response is a stern rebuke. The message is clear—our master wants us to be wise stewards of what he's given us. But the part we often miss is this: to create a return, we also have to be willing to receive. If the servants had responded to the master by saying, "I'm really doing fine. I can just use the talents I have," then they wouldn't have been able to give him a return on his investment and bring joy to his heart as well.

It's a paradox: receiving is about you and not about you all at the same time.

To keep this perspective, it's helpful to know how we want to invest the deposits we're intentionally making in our lives or the ways we're open to receiving from others and God. If we only think about the first part (ourselves) but not who will benefit in the end (the kingdom and others), then deposits in our emotional bank accounts will continue to make us feel guilty.

For example: "I will make a deposit in my emotional account by taking fifteen minutes alone each day (if you stop there then you're likely to feel guilty) *so that* I can be a more energetic wife, mom, and friend" (there's the return on the investment—for your family, the kingdom, and you).

Let's give it a try:

○ I will make a deposit in my emotional account by

_____

_____

○ so that

_____

_____

Ask yourself:

> Why am I doing this?
>
> Who will it benefit in the end?
>
> How will I make sure it happens?

When God looks at his daughters, he sees each of us the same. He wants us to love ourselves the way we love others in our lives. It grieves him when we treat ourselves poorly, just like it would if we treated one of our sisters in Christ that way. If someone were harsh or demanding with a close friend of yours, you would come to her defense. If she were exhausted or burned out, you would try to help her get some rest. Sometimes we need to do the same for ourselves. Telling women they're not allowed to receive is one of the subtlest and most dangerous tactics of the enemy. He might not be able to make us ineffective by getting us to fall into a major sin, but he can accomplish the same thing by driving us to become utterly empty and exhausted.

You are worth investing in, sweet sister. You are a daughter of the King, a holy princess, a woman with a purpose in this world and a calling on your life. You are of infinite value, and no one can take your place. You're our one shot at what you have to offer. God doesn't have a backup plan for you. So take care of yourself. You're blessing all of us when you do, and you bring joy to the heart of God too.

Your Personal Investment Plan

Everything we've talked about comes down to one thing: love. The end goal of taking care of ourselves isn't simply to be happy or personally satisfied. It's so that we can love God, others, and ourselves.

It's okay to take care of yourself because you are someone's beloved. You are the bride of Christ. You belong to the One who hung the stars in place, who knows every detail of your day, who is waiting for the moment when you're finally together forever. You matter to him. He wants the best for you.

If you haven't figured it out yet: *you're amazing because you're God's creation and he lives in you.* You're valuable because you belong to him. You're worth investing in because he paid the ultimate price for you.

Dare to take the risk. Love yourself because he loves you.

We live busy lives. Making deposits in our emotional bank account takes planning and being intentional. It may take our bank sending us an "overdrawn account notice" before we realize we've spent a bit too much. In much the same way, many of us wait until we're burned out before we realize how drained we are emotionally.

I've been there. In *Leading on Empty*, Wayne Cordeiro explains how God has wired our bodies. He's given our brains a supply of serotonin, a chemical that gives us a feeling of well-being. When we're in chronic stress, those levels get used up. So our bodies switch to the backup plan: adrenaline. Think of it like the little bit of money you set aside in case of emergencies. But we can only live on that for so long. When that supply is depleted, we truly are "in the red"—physically, emotionally, and often spiritually.

At that point we need serious restoration. That happens through rest and also intentional deposits. If we get to the point of being totally overdrawn, it can take six months to a year to restore our serotonin levels. By proactively making deposits ahead of time, we can ensure we don't get to that point. We keep our emotional bank accounts full so that when there is an unexpected expense, we have enough to cover it.

· · · · · · **Creating Your Personal Investment Plan** · · · · · ·

In each of the areas below, brainstorm ways to be renewed. *These are not goals.* They shouldn't make you feel pressure or as if they are something you must do. These are deposits in your bank account—not withdrawals. For example, social might be "coffee with a friend" and physical might be "taking a walk on a nice afternoon to enjoy God's creation." Use the deposit list you made earlier in this chapter as a starting place and then add anything else that comes to mind. Take a few moments to ask God to show you how he made you and what you really need.

Also, if you don't enjoy it, then don't do it. The reason? While we need to push through and do hard things out of discipline in our lives (and you probably have those on your "Do What You Can Plan"), those won't maintain or rebuild your serotonin levels. That only happens when you're doing something you enjoy. If you're feeling guilty right now, remember, this is about *receiving so that you can invest.*

Here's an example in each area to get you started:

- ◦ Emotional—Watching a movie that makes me laugh
- ◦ Mental—Reading a book I really enjoy
- ◦ Spiritual—Writing a page in my prayer journal
- ◦ Social—A "girls' night out" with friends
- ◦ Physical—Walking the dog

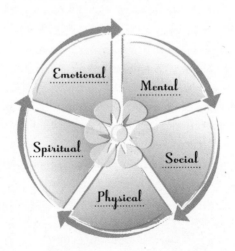

· · · · · · · · · **Ultimate Goal: Invest in LIFE** · · · · · · · ·

"Love the Lord your God with all your heart and with all your
soul and with all your mind and with all your strength. . . .
Love your neighbor as yourself." There is no commandment
greater than these. (Mark 12:30–31)

What's of Greatest Worth?

Think back to the parable of the talents we talked about earlier in
this chapter. When the master returns and praises the servants,
he says six words that are of the greatest worth in our lives: "Well
done, good and faithful servant!" (Matt. 25:23).

That's what it's all about in the end: receiving and then investing so that one day we too can hear from the lips of the One our
hearts love, "Well done."

You are valuable.

And you have so much of value to offer.

Take care of you.

And finish well.

11

What God Really Wants Your Heart to Remember

I call you. "Can we meet for coffee again? There are some things I want to remind you of just one more time."

We talk of what we've been through together in these chapters—of discovering more about who we are and who God made us to be.

We laugh, sip from our cups, and smile, maybe even shed a tear or two.

"It's been a good journey," I say, "and there are some things I want you to carry with you always. I think the One who loves you does too."

I pull a box from under the table. It has a big, fluffy bow on top and a ribbon around it.

You clap your hands. "Is that for me?"

"Of course!" I declare.

You slip off the ribbon and gently left the lid.

You pull out the piece of paper and run your hand along the edges. It looks like it belongs to you, with you—like it was made *just for you.*

You read the words at the top aloud, slowly: "What God Really Wants Your Heart to Remember."

Sip by sip, line by line, we talk through each phrase on the page together . . .

You Really Were Made for More Than This

I understand how it works when you read a book like this. You close the last page with good intentions. Then the phone rings, the kids throw spaghetti, the dog eats your new shoes, and you wonder what in the world just happened.

Your heart cries, "I thought I was made for more than this."

You quiet that voice quickly and tell yourself to stop feeling that way.

But the truth is, you *were* made for more than this.

You *are* made for more than this.

The trouble isn't feeling that way—it's expecting it all to happen here. That discontent within you is a homing beacon, reminding you of Eden and redirecting you toward heaven. The disappointment only comes when we expect all of the *more* we're promised in the then and there to happen in the here and now.

"He has made everything beautiful in its time. He has also set eternity in the human heart; yet no one can fathom what God has done from beginning to end" (Eccles. 3:11).

We hold eternity in our hearts—all we've been, all we will be—and we don't understand it. How can we? All we feel is that longing, that ache within us.

So we try to change our circumstances. We alter this or that. We want things to be different. But that longing never really goes away.

It won't completely.

Not this side of heaven.

What we've been talking about isn't making our lives perfect. Instead it's about learning to turn to Jesus when our hearts feel restless, to have the courage to be who he made us here and now no matter what, to cross the finish line into everything he has for us in eternity with a smile on our faces, knowing we ran well every step of the way.

When we tell ourselves, "I was made for more, so I'm going to . . . run off to Jamaica, start a new relationship, switch to another job for the hundredth time," we miss what that ache inside us means.

When we stifle that longing and say, "I wasn't made for more, so I'll just settle for this forever," we do the same. That leads us to be apathetic and miss out on the joy, adventure, and good plans God does have for us in this life.

The hard line we walk is this: "I was made for more—more of Jesus, more of who he created me to be, more of his purpose for my life, more of his love flowing through me—and I'm going to pursue that with all my heart. But I also realize that I won't have all he has for me until I step into eternity. I'm not going to let that get me off track. I'm going to keep going and remember that 'The path of the righteous is like the morning sun, shining ever brighter till the full light of day' (Prov. 4:18)."

If you feel that "I was made for more" feeling again even after all the hard work you've done in this book, don't let it make you think you're missing something or you've done it wrong. Just let it be a reminder that you're not home yet . . . but you're on your way. And you're getting a little closer every day.

> *Oh, yes, you're made for more . . .*
> *more than the worry, the weariness, the*
> *what-has-to-get-done.*
> *You're made for more . . .*
> *more of Jesus, more of His presence in your life, more of all He*
> *has to offer.*
> *Joy, hope, peace, grace, goodness.*

And right there in the middle of it all is you,
beautiful you,
deeply loved, chosen, called,
and on your way Home
to the One who cherishes you
so much more
than your heart can even know.

You Really Were Made for Right Here, Right Now Too

Our hearts pull us toward home as they whisper, "You were made for more than this," and yet we're also made for this moment. Out of all of history, God chose this time for you to be on earth. He knew the exact second you would enter this world with a cry and change it forever.

In between the laundry, the endless trips to the office, the mundane parts of being human, we can forget that we're part of a bigger story, a greater plan.

And here's the thing: we only get one you. There never has been, and never will be, another you in this world. God doesn't have a backup plan or replacement policy. That's why I feel so passionately about you being who you are and embracing it. We don't need a copy of someone else—we need the one and only, original you.

How do we live in this place, suspended between history and eternity? How do we find the courage to offer who we are in the middle of the mess? My dear friend and fellow writer Ann Voskamp leads the way in her book *One Thousand Gifts*:

> Time is a relentless river. It rages on, a respecter of no one. And this, this is the only way to slow time: When I fully enter time's swift current, enter into the current moment with the weight of all my attention. I slow the torrent with the weight of me all here. I can slow the torrent by being all here. I only live the full life when I live fully in the moment.[1]

Ann says this present moment is the only place we can fully EXPERIENCE God because he is *I Am*. We find him not in the future or in the past. Instead we find him right here with us, beside us, in us. When we take hold of that, take hold of him, then we become all we're called to be today.

We may think back with regret on who we wish we'd been. We may look forward with fear about who we might (or might not) become. But the only place where we can offer ourselves, where God can use us, is the moment we're in right now.

Living that way requires awareness and intention. I hope our journey together has helped you gain a bit more of both. What you have to give, what you have to share with the world, is far too important to be missed. We need you to be you—not tomorrow, next week, or next year but where you are at this very second.

The temptation will always be to say, "After I . . ." or "When this happens, then I'll . . . ," but life doesn't work that way. You, your circumstances, your life will never be everything you want them to be. Don't let that stop you.

Embrace this moment. Be who you are. You're the best gift you can give the world.

> I'm thinking of you today . . .
> the past pulling at your sleeves,
> the future tugging at your hands.
> Take a deep breath.
> Just for a moment.
> Just in *this* moment.
> Ah, yes, look at you—
> beautiful you.
> The sunlight of *now*
> is on your face,
> the glow within you is spilling out too.

That's the thing about light—
we can't save it up
or carry it back.
It's always for now,
always for where we are today,
because it flows from the One
who is I Am.
We can only reflect Him in the here and now
because that's where He is.
Yes?
So keep shining, girl . . .
and know the world is better, brighter for it.

All You Are Really Can Be Used for Good

If we really were sitting at a table in a coffee shop, I imagine a straw would be somewhere nearby. At this point, I'd reach for it and hold it up in the air between us, my fingers grasping the middle. Then I'd say, "As the saying goes, 'Every stick has two ends.' The core characteristics about us are like that too."

By this point you might tease me, "You and all of your analogies!"

I'd grin and point to one end of the straw.

"See this end? That represents our characteristics acted out as strengths. For example, when I'm living in tune with God, my sensitivity looks like compassion."

Then I'd touch the other end of the stick. "But on my own, it drifts the other way and becomes anxiety."

I don't believe God wants us to throw out the "sticks" in our lives. He just wants us to move toward the end that is more like him. The same Paul who ended up writing to the early churches started out being belligerent, overzealous, and an oppressive leader. After Jesus appeared to him, Paul was determined, enthusiastic, and an encouraging leader. Same characteristics—different ends of the stick.

I've watched women (including myself) work hard to remove parts of themselves that God deliberately placed within them. It's a painful process that usually doesn't get us very far. Instead of eliminating, it seems God's goal is more that we simply surrender and obey as we are.

In the times when we can't seem to transform our weaknesses to strengths, God can still make up for (and even use!) our imperfections. Judy, a reader on my blog *Heart to Heart with Holley*, shared this story:

> God used a speaker, an ordinary, everyday woman (translated: just like me) whose voice quivered as she spoke to help me. Normally when I pick up on nervousness in a public speaker it makes me nervous for them. But this time God used it to speak to my heart. The thought He brought to mind was if the message the speaker shared about Christ meant so much to her that she was willing to endure nervousness, I could brave the fear of what He was asking me to do, too, because the message is worth it.
>
> When I had a chance to meet with the speaker a few days later, she mentioned that her nervousness hindered the message. I gratefully told her that her nervousness was the very thing God used to help me be at peace with myself and say yes to what He was asking me to do.[2]

God really can use all of you—strengths, weaknesses, imperfections, and challenges. The only time that can't happen is when we refuse to give an area of our lives to him. But whatever we place in his hands, he can lovingly make into something useful and even beautiful. Like that straw, we can experience his love flowing through *every* part of our lives if we'll just open ourselves to him.

All you are,
everything God created you to be,
becomes a gift when placed in His hands.
There's nothing He can't mold, shape, redeem,
form into something beautiful.
You don't have to be afraid or hold back—
just hold out your heart to the One who promises
to complete the good work He's already started in you.

All Things Really Are Possible for You

I'm sure you remember the story of Peter walking on water with Jesus. Peter starts off well, takes a few steps, and begins to sink.

Jesus asks, "Why did you doubt?" (Matt. 14:31).

I pause and ponder, "Who did Peter doubt? Jesus or himself?" And it seems there's a whisper in response . . .

Same thing.

What I mean is this: "I no longer live, but Christ lives in me" (Gal. 2:20).

I'm still quick to protest, "But I have so many weaknesses!" And then I remember that every promise given and every truth declared was for us, all of us, and none of us have it together. Our humanity isn't too much for God. "Many are the plans in a person's heart, but it is the LORD's purpose that prevails" (Prov. 19:21). There is nothing God can't do through a heart fully surrendered to him.

Nothing.

Lead an entire nation through a desert.

Knock down a giant with a single stone.

Fulfill his purpose for your life.

Let's believe that in us, through us, in spite of us, "With God all things are possible" (Matt. 19:26).

What does this sound like in our everyday lives? "This seems impossible for me. But nothing is impossible for the God who lives in me. That means all things really are possible for me too. I can do this with him."

Good news:

Nothing is impossible for you
because all things are possible for the God who lives in you.
There's no obstacle too great, no wall too high, no valley too low.
You can get through it, over it, beyond it together.
With Him, you have more than enough . . .
you have everything you need
and you're everything you need to be
for His purposes to prevail in your life.

What You Have to Offer Really Is Enough

One morning I thought of all I had to do, all the hearts I felt called to love, all the words I want to share with the world.

I felt very small and the need felt so very big.

Then it seemed God whispered, "Just offer what you have. I will make up the difference."

Yes, of course!

The loaves and fish.

You know that story. It's the one where Jesus is teaching a huge, hungry crowd, and there's nothing to feed them. All anyone has to offer is five loaves and two fish. But put those in the hands of Jesus, and "They all ate and were satisfied, and the disciples picked up twelve basketfuls of broken pieces of bread and fish" (Mark 6:42–43).

Yes, in the hands of Jesus a little is a lot, *even more than we need.*

I don't always approach it that way.

Instead I try to change the bread. I think, "Well, her bread is golden and gorgeous. If I can just make my loaves like hers, then what I have will be enough."

Or I tell myself, "I just need to decorate the bread! I'll draw the Mona Lisa on top with frosting. If I can just make my loaves perfect, then what I have will be enough."

Maybe you, my fellow traveler on this journey, might do this too?

But Jesus steps in, takes us by the hands, looks into our hearts, and says, "Daughter, you don't have to be enough or have a lot. Only offer all you are, all you have, to me. I will turn that into abundance beyond all you can imagine. All things are possible with me."

Not only is Jesus the supplier—he is the multiplier too.

It's not about what we have to offer. It's about whose hands we place it in.

And those hands? We can place our hearts safely there too.

> Hey, you, the one with those "loaves and fish,"
> wondering if what you have to offer can even make a difference.
> Oh, yes, it can.
> We need you, just you, to open your hands and your heart
> to dare to give what you've been given,
> to place it in the hands of the One who made you
> and who can make what you have to offer
> more than enough too.

You Really Can Live Differently

Our journey together has been all about believing we're amazing just as we are and pressing on toward all God has for us too.

The hardest part of moving forward for me isn't taking the next step, finding courage, overcoming obstacles. No, the biggest challenge has been the voice inside my mind. It's the one that says, "You can never do this. This is in the way. That won't ever change."

You've struggled with that too? We're not the only ones.

As Priscilla Shirer says in her book *One in a Million: Journey to Your Promised Land*, the Israelites also battled fear and insecurities:

> If there's a single word that doomed this generation of God's people from experiencing Promised Land living in their lifetime, it's this one: "nevertheless."
>
> They had heard with their own ears the assurances of God. They had seen and certainly tasted the cluster of fruit that more than verified, beyond their wildest imaginations, just how accurate God had been when He had described the land to them. . . .
>
> Nevertheless.[3]

She goes on to say that we're all tempted to do the same. I discover her words as I sit on my back porch one evening. As I finish, I lean back and stare into the deep summer sky.

I ask God, "What do I say instead?"

And like shooting stars, two words blaze across my mind.

Even so.

Yes, the situation is difficult and the obstacles seem insurmountable. Even so, God will deliver me.

Yes, I left my comfort zone about a hundred miles ago, and all I want to do is eat a vat of chocolate. Even so, God can use me.

Yes, it feels like the valley is dark, the mountains are high, and the enemy is strong. Even so, God is able to get me to the Promised Land.

Even so.

Those two little words don't deny the difficulties or paste on a smile that says, "Everything is fine." They acknowledge life is hard. They recognize the obstacles. But in the end, they shift our gaze from what we see to who we know. And that changes everything—especially us.

You've begun to move forward, to make changes, to recognize the incredible woman you are and become more of who God created you to be. And the enemy would love nothing more than to convince you it's too much, you can't do it, there's not enough time . . . the list is endless. But it's not true, dear friend. You can change. You can grow. You already have—don't let anything stand in your way.

Yours is not a life of "nevertheless."

It's one of "even so."

> *Are you ready to take that next step?*
> *You can do this, sweet girl.*
> *With Him.*
> *In His power.*
> *That power created the world,*
> *spoke the stars into place,*
> *spread the sea from one shore to another.*
> *That's the power that lives in YOU.*
> *Move forward in faith,*
> *into all you are and all He has for you.*
> *You're already on your way.*

You Really Are Loved More Than You Know

I grew up in Houston, close to NASA. The evening news often contained talk about the latest mission or plans for venturing even deeper into the universe. Over the years it seemed this became clear: the more we discover about space, the more we realize how little we know. I paused to look up from my computer at the sky just now. The blue stretches far beyond my ability to see. It reminds me of this verse: "For as high as the heavens are above the earth, so great is his love for those who fear him" (Ps. 103:11).

As high as the heavens are above the earth. How high is that? Endless. That's the way God's love for us is too.

In *The Truman Show*, Jim Carrey plays a man whose entire life is a reality show. From the day he was born, everything in his life has been a performance without him even realizing it. Everything around him responds based on what he does. Our lives can feel that way too—when we mess up, it can feel as if the sky is going to crash down around us. But as much as it may seem like it, our lives aren't about us. They're about our Maker. And his love never changes. Yes, we can separate ourselves from fellowship with God because of the choices we make. But we can't stop him from loving us.

The apostle Paul says, "I pray that you, being rooted and established in love, may have power, together with all the Lord's holy people, to grasp how wide and long and high and deep is the love of Christ, and to know this love that surpasses knowledge—that you may be filled to the measure of all the fullness of God" (Eph. 3:17–19).

It seems Paul is praying for us to know how high the sky is, and that's impossible. But wait—one phrase stands out to me in this verse: "to know this love that surpasses knowledge" (v. 19). When the word "know" is used in a biblical context, it is often associated with intimacy. For example, "Adam knew Eve" is a polite description of their physical relationship. We can't ever comprehend the love of God, but Paul's prayer, and mine too, is for us to experience it in our daily lives in a powerful way.

Embracing God's love is done not with our heads but with our hearts.

It's not about understanding but instead about simply receiving.

We spend a lot of time trying to figure out how God can love us and what that means. But all we really need to know is that he does.

Really.

Truly.

Just as you are.
As high as the sky.
More than you can even imagine.

> *You're loved.*
> *More than you know.*
> *More than you see.*
> *Deeper than you've even dared to dream.*
> *All that you fear holds you back*
> *has been wiped away, forgiven,*
> *covered up by grace.*
> *And the One who created you,*
> *knows you, calls you His own*
> *looks at you with love*
> *and says, "You're mine forever."*
> *Your heart has a home—*
> *and it's not a place*
> *but a Person who will never let you go.*

There Really Is a Good Plan for Your Life

A few years ago, my husband and I set out on a hike with a few friends. I expected it to be easy. But as the miles wore on, the hill grew steeper, and more obstacles appeared, I began to wonder what I'd gotten myself into by agreeing to go.

At one point, my athletic husband disappeared around a curve ahead in the trail. He'd told us he would go ahead of us and scout out the trail. But as the minutes ticked by, I began to worry. Where was he? Why hadn't he come back for us? What was really in front of us?

Just then we broke through some trees and found ourselves standing on a beautiful overlook. The entire valley stretched below us. My grinning husband pointed out landmarks below that we'd passed. "See," he said, "that's the stream we crossed. There's the place we stopped for water. Those are the rocks we had to climb over."

And as I looked back on where we'd come from, it all made sense. That winding trail through the woods was a clear, wide ribbon. Those places I'd wondered about were just stops along the trail. Having arrived at our destination, I could look back and say, "Oh, yes, that was so worth it."

Our lives can be like that too. We go through each day and make a little more progress. We face obstacles, grow weary, and wonder when things will really get better. It may even seem as if God is nowhere to be found. Where are we headed? Why is it worth it to keep going?

But God promises us that in the end it will all be worth it and we'll understand everything we went through along the way. Jeremiah 29:11 says God has good plans for us, a hope and a future. Does that mean it will always be easy or what we want? Nope, not at all. What it does mean is that we can trust him—no matter what.

I imagine one day we'll stand before Jesus in heaven and we'll look back over our lives with a different perspective. The moments you lived in your strengths, the challenges you pushed through, the ways you made a difference—they'll all be something beautiful that you can give the One who gave everything for you.

Hello, you . . .
wondering what's next,
where you're headed,
what might happen now.
There's One who knows the way.
Every step.
Every day.
Every moment.

He never promised it would be easy
but He did promise you'll never be alone.
He has a plan for your life, your heart,
and it's good.
Better than you hoped.
Better than you dreamed.
More than you can even imagine.

. . . And You Really Are Amazing

My imagination is shifting back to that coffee shop. By now the sun has slipped lower in the sky, and our cups have long been empty.

I look at you and smile. "Thanks for spending this time with me."

A waitress comes and clears our table. She pauses for a moment and asks, "Can I get you anything else?"

I smile and answer, "I think we've got all we need."

And it's true: "His divine power has given us everything we need for life and godliness" (2 Pet. 1:3 NIV 1984).

You had all you need before you ever read the first page of this book. You're already amazing because God made you, formed you, and lives within you. You're amazing because you belong to him, because he has a plan for your life, because with him there's nothing you can't do.

I hope our time together has given you some new tools, let God whisper some truths to your heart, and offered you some courage to take the next steps into all he has for you. But before we ever crossed paths, you had everything you need. You still do. You always will.

I don't know what you'll do after you close this book. Maybe you'll walk over to a crib and pick up a baby newly awakened from a nap. Maybe you'll finish a lunch break and step into a meeting. Maybe you'll uncurl from the couch, grab your keys, and head into your day.

Whatever it is, I know that you have what it takes to accomplish God's purpose for your life.

I know that the people whose paths you cross are going to be blessed because of you.

I know that your life is a story being written by an Author who has more in store for you than either of us can even imagine. Thank you for letting me share a few pages of it with you.

This isn't the end.

With the God who makes you amazing, it's always only the beginning.

Go Deeper Guide
(for Individuals and Groups)

In addition to the questions below, visit www.holleygerth.com for more tools, encouraging content, and even life coaching opportunities.

Chapter 1:
A Heart-to-Heart Talk

1. If you had coffee with a close friend today and she asked how you were *really* doing, what would you say?

2. Which story at the beginning of the chapter did you relate to the most (the friend at lunch, counseling client, or woman sending the email)?

3. The "it girl" is thought of as a woman everyone wants to be like in our culture. Do you ever feel pressure to be like women in the media? Share one example.

_____

_____

4. In contrast, through Scripture God says you're an "is girl." He looks at you and says, "She is_____." Fill in the blank with a few of the words your heart most needs to hear today. (Example: She is <u>loved</u>.)

_____

_____

5. We sometimes feel shame about who we are or what we do. We tell ourselves, "Most people don't . . ." But those very things can be important parts of the unique way God has created us to make a difference in the world. What are those for you? Finish this sentence below: "Most people don't, but I . . ."

_____

_____

6. We all have brokenness in our lives, and that can keep us from seeing who we really are in Christ or believing he can use us. Write a short prayer asking God to heal your heart and make something unexpectedly beautiful out of your hurts.

_____

_____

7. One of the most powerful passages of Scripture about who God made us to be and how intimately he knows us is found in Psalm 139. Read it and write a short prayer that includes a few phrases from it below (if you're in a group, take time to pray for each other too).

_____

_____

Chapter 2: Who Am I, REALLY?

1. Look back to the strengths you circled on the list in this chapter. Write your top three here.

   _____

   _____

2. If you haven't already, put them through the STRENGTH test below.

Service	*Does it help me serve God and others?*
Time	*Has it been present throughout much of my life?*
Relationships	*Do others see this?*
Energy	*Do I feel energized when I'm living this way?*
Natural	*Does this come naturally to me most of the time? Or do I know God has intentionally developed this in me even though it doesn't?*
Glory	*Does God ultimately get the glory from it?*
Trials	*Even in hard times, does it usually come through somehow?*
Heart	*Does this really feel like a core part of who I am?*

3. We often think of weaknesses as a negative thing. But research shows that having weaknesses in certain areas actually helps us to be stronger in others. God also says that his "strength is made perfect in weakness" (2 Cor. 12:9 NKJV). What's a weakness you wish you didn't have? In what ways could it actually help you be who God created you to be? (Example: Being weak at details helps make you strong at seeing the big picture.)

   _____

   _____

4. Look back to the skills list in this chapter. Write your top three here.

_____

_____

_____

5. Skills circles can help us see how our skills support our core strengths. Try drawing one here (look back to the example in the chapter if you need help).

6. Social circles help us understand who is in our life and how we're connected to them. You began thinking about that in this chapter; now you have time to actually write some names in each of the circles below. (If you need a reminder of what each circle means, look back to the definitions in the chapter.)

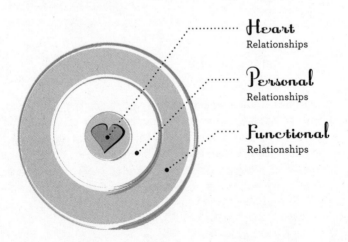

𝓗𝓮𝓪𝓻𝓽
Relationships

𝓟𝓮𝓻𝓼𝓸𝓷𝓪𝓵
Relationships

𝓕𝓾𝓷𝓬𝓽𝓲𝓸𝓷𝓪𝓵
Relationships

7. Look back to the "Find Your Who" exercise in this chapter. If you haven't already, fill in the blanks. When you look at your answers, who does it seem God most wants you to use your strengths and skills to serve? Write a short prayer asking him to use you in new ways (if you're in a group, take time to pray for each other too).

Chapter 3: Why Is It So Hard to Believe I'm Amazing?

1. Lie #1: "I have to be perfect." How does knowing "by one sacrifice he has made perfect forever those who are being made holy" (Heb. 10:14) change that for you? What does God want us to pursue instead of perfection?

----

2. Lie #2: "I need to be more like her." Who do you tend to compare yourself to? What helps you focus on who you are in Christ instead?

----

3. Lie #3: "I don't have anything to offer." What keeps you from "putting your truffles on the table" for God and others? If you had no fear about the worth of what you had to share with the world, what would you do?

----

4. Lie #4: "Being confident will make me prideful and selfish." What's the difference between insecurity and humility?

_____

_____

5. Lie #5: "I am who others say I am." What have others said to you that has impacted the way you see yourself? What does God say about you instead?

_____

_____

6. Are there any other lies you've become aware of that you need God to replace with the truth? Write them below.

_____

_____

7. Write a short prayer asking God to continue revealing any lies in your life and to lead you into the truth about who you really are in him (if you're in a group, take time to pray for each other too).

_____

_____

_____

Chapter 4: Why Do I Feel This Way?

1. Are you dominated more by your head or heart? Look back to the descriptions about both and write a few phrases that sound most like you.

_____

_____

_____

2. Emotions make great messengers but bad bosses. What helps you make sure you're ultimately obeying God rather than your feelings?

3. Which description most fits your family growing up—stuffers, screamers, or surfers? What parts of your emotional history still fit you well and which ones have you outgrown?

4. We talked about having an emotional range and how if we don't allow ourselves to experience negative emotions, then we limit our ability to experience positive ones as well. Are there any experiences in your life that have caused you to shut off part of your heart? If so, write a short prayer sharing them with God and asking him to heal you and free you to feel again (if you're in a group, take time to talk to God together and pray for each other).

5. Look at the list of emotions in this chapter. Which ones are you most comfortable expressing? Which ones are you least comfortable expressing?

6. Read the story of Joshua and Caleb in Numbers 14:1–9. They chose faith over feelings and were the only ones to see the Promised Land. What's one thing they did that you can apply to your life?

7. "Above all else, guard your heart, for it is the wellspring of life" (Prov. 4:23 NIV 1984). What's one specific way you can guard your heart this week? Write a short prayer asking God to help you do so (if you're in a group, take time to pray for each other too).

Chapter 5: Where Am I Going?

1. Egypt: Are there any areas in your life where you feel like you're in Egypt? What is God prompting you to do so you can move on from that place?

2. Encamped: Are there any areas in your life where you feel like you're encamped? Review the reasons in the chapter why God sometimes has us stay put for a while. Which one did you identify with and why?

3. Setting out: Which one of the profiles in this section (settler, explorer, traveler) did you relate to most? What's the next step God is asking you to take in an area of your life?

4. The Promised Land: Are there any areas in your life where you feel like you're in the Promised Land? What are you doing to possess, defend, and enjoy it?

5. If you didn't do so in the chapter, fill in your Life Map below:

· · · · · · · · · · · · · *My Life Map* · · · · · · · · · · · · · ·

Under each section draw a dot and write the areas of your life that fit in each one.

Promised Land

Egypt

Encamped

Setting Out

6. None of us are intended to go through life alone. Who encourages you on your journey? Who else might be willing to do so?

7. Based on where you are now, write a short prayer asking God to help you take the next step in his plan for your life (if you're in a group, take time to pray for each other too).

Chapter 6: Who's with Me?

1. Do you ever feel lonely or out of place? What are the lies the enemy tries to whisper to your heart when that happens, and what's the truth?

2. The word for "helper" in the Bible that describes Eve is the same word often used when God helps us. When you thought of Eve being called a "helper" before now, what did you think it meant? How does seeing that word in this context change that?

3. What makes you afraid that you won't be loved? Do you ever hide from others? Describe a time when you overcame your fear and found the courage to reach out instead.

4. "Love all. Please One." What's the difference between loving someone and trying to please them?

5. There's a "Safe Person Checklist" in this chapter based on 1 Corinthians 13:1–8. Take a moment to read that passage. Who are the safe people in your life?

6. As daughters of Eve, we all struggle with the desire for control—we just display it in different ways. In the descriptions of internal and external control, which one could you most relate to? What helps you let go of control and trust God so that you can freely love?

7. This quote by C. S. Lewis is powerful:

> To love at all is to be vulnerable. Love anything, and your heart will certainly be wrung and possibly broken. If you want to make sure of keeping it intact, you must give your heart to no one, not even to an animal. Wrap it carefully round with hobbies and little luxuries; avoid all entanglements; lock it up safe in the casket or coffin of your selfishness. But in that casket—safe, dark, motionless, airless—it will change. It will not be broken; it will become unbreakable, impenetrable, irredeemable.[1]

If loving is so risky, why does God ask us to do it? Write a short prayer asking him for the courage to love (if you're in a group, take time to pray for each other too).

Chapter 7: How Do I Connect?

1. Have you ever thought of the ways you connect with others as strengths God has given you? What are some ways that others frequently describe the way you connect with them (for example, outgoing, compassionate, fun, kind)?

---

2. Which setting (one-to-one, one-to-few, one-to-many) are you most drawn to? Describe your favorite way to spend time with other people.

---

3. Which structure seems to fit you best (leading, partnering, serving)? Describe a situation in which you used this to help others.

_____

_____

_____

4. When it comes to sight, are you more internal or external? Write down some phrases in the description that sound most like you.

_____

_____

5. Which sphere of needs does your heart feel called to most (intellectual, relational, emotional, practical)? Describe a time when God used you to meet a need in that way.

_____

_____

6. We are all part of the body of Christ. Read 1 Corinthians 12:12–31. If you were to choose a part of the body that you feel best represents you, what would it be and why? (Example: "Hands, because I love to reach out and serve.")

_____

_____

7. Good news: we don't have to rely on ourselves to live in our strengths or deal with our weaknesses. "For God did not give us a spirit of timidity, but a spirit of power, of love and of self-discipline" (2 Tim. 1:7 NIV 1984). What's a specific way you can apply this verse in your life this week? Write a short prayer asking for God's help to do so (if you're in a group, take time to pray for each other too).

_____

_____

_____

Chapter 8: What Does God Want Me to Do with My Life?

1. Most of us have busy schedules. What's the difference between "life to the full" and simply "a full life"?

   _____

   _____

2. If you have not done so already, take time to write your LIFE statement here:

   I am created and called to express my faith through love, especially by

   _____

   _____

   (verb ending in "ing" + what + who + how)

   If you've already written it, make any changes that come to mind.

3. Expectations are like laws we place on ourselves. "You are not under the law, but under grace" (Rom. 6:14). Write some of the expectations you feel below:

   I must_____ or this will happen: _____.

   I must_____ or this will happen: _____.

   I must_____ or this will happen: _____.

   Where are those expectations coming from? What does God want to replace them with instead?

   _____

   _____

4. If you knew you would be completely loved and accepted no matter what, then which items would you cross off your (mental or actual) to-do list?

5. When you read your LIFE statement, what would you like to add to your to-do list instead?

6. In Matthew 22:34–40, Jesus shares what matters most to God. Read that passage and paraphrase it in your own words below.

7. Write a short prayer asking God to help you live your LIFE statement more fully (if you're in a group, take time to pray for each other too).

Chapter 9: What Are My Next Steps?

1. "Let us throw off everything that hinders and the sin that so easily entangles. And let us run with perseverance the race marked out for us, fixing our eyes on Jesus, the pioneer and perfecter of our faith" (Heb. 12:1–2). What tends to hinder and/or entangle you?

2. What did you think of the "Do What You Can Plan"? Which aspect stood out to you most? Describe a time when God prompted you to make a change in your life and you did it. What helped you?

3. If you didn't fill out your "Do What You Can Plan" in the chapter, you can do so now:

Change God wants me to make:	Small next step:	How I'll celebrate:

4. How will these changes help you live your LIFE?

5. What's your strategy for dealing with slipups and setbacks in your plan?

6. Which organizational personality sounds most like you? Write down some phrases that stood out to you in the descriptions.

7. Write a short prayer asking God to help you make these changes and move forward in all he has for you (if you're in a group, take time to pray for each other too).

_____

_____

_____

Chapter 10: Is It Okay to Take Care of Myself?

1. Write down more deposits/withdrawals in your emotional bank account:

Withdrawals *(things that take emotional energy in my life right now)*	Deposits *(things that increase/restore my emotional energy in my life right now)*
Example: Conflict with my teenage daughter	*Example: Coffee with a dear friend*

2. Why is it so hard for many women to receive? Which of the common reasons listed in this chapter did you most relate to personally?

_____

_____

3. What fills you up and brings you joy?

_____

_____

4. Think of the people in your life. Who encourages you the most?

   ....

   ....

5. We receive so that we can invest in the kingdom and others. Try starting to make a receive/invest plan below:

   I will make a deposit in my emotional account by

   ....

   ....

   so that

   ....

   ....

   Ask yourself:
   Why am I doing this?
   Who will it benefit in the end?
   How will I make sure it happens?

6. It's important to be intentional about receiving just as we are about giving. If you haven't already done the Personal Investment Plan in the chapter, do so here. If you have, add a few more ideas.

   ....

   ....

   ....

   In each of the areas below, brainstorm more ways to be renewed. Here's an example in each area to get you started:

   - Emotional—Watching a movie that makes me laugh
   - Mental—Reading a book I really enjoy
   - Spiritual—Writing a page in my prayer journal
   - Social—A "girls' night out" with friends
   - Physical—Walking the dog

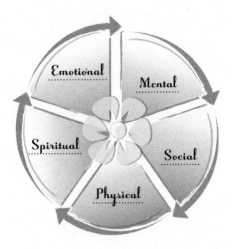

"Love the Lord your God with all your heart and with all your soul and with all your mind and with all your strength.... Love your neighbor as yourself." There is no commandment greater than these. (Mark 12:30–31)

7. Write a short prayer thanking God for all he's given you and asking him to help you receive from him and others all that you need (if you're in a group, take time to pray for each other too).

Chapter 11: What God Really Wants Your Heart to Remember

1. As you think about making changes in your life, what is your greatest fear or obstacle? What can help you with it?

2. What are the "loaves and fish" you want to offer Jesus? What would you like to see him do with the gifts and strengths he's given you?

3. What's one new truth you've learned about how much God loves you through this book?

4. Do you ever feel "I was made for more than this"? What do you think of the idea that those thoughts are intended to point us toward heaven?

5. What helps you make the most of every moment in this life? What would you do if you knew you couldn't fail?

6. How do you see yourself differently now than when you started this journey?

7. Write a short prayer expressing your heart to God and asking him to show you what's next on your journey with him (if you're in a group, take time to pray for each other too).

Acknowledgments

The more I write, the more I realize it's about so much more than words on a page. It's really about a beautiful community of people joining together to birth something into the world.

Mark, thank you for helping me become the woman God created me to be and reminding me of who I really am even on the hard days. I love you.

Thanks to my family (especially Mom, Dad, Stephen, Amber, Granny Eula, Grandpa Red, and Poppi) for showing me that words are a way of loving that can truly make a difference.

Chip MacGregor, you are more than an agent. You're also a wise friend, a valued advisor, and one of the first who caught the vision. Thank you.

Jennifer Leep—every time I think of how God gave you to me as my editor at Revell, I still get happy tears in my eyes. Your insight, friendship, and support have meant more to me than I can even express. I'm so glad we get to do this together.

Twila Bennett, you are the queen of marketing, and I'm so thrilled to have found a new friend as well as a wonderful partner on this project in you. We are like a pair of cute shoes at our favorite store (you know the one). The perfect match.

The DaySpring Team—I am so blessed to do ministry and business with you. I'm especially grateful to Bill Couey, Donna Estes, Jesse Lane, Kim Marquette, Katie Matzenbacher, Lainie Button, Linn Carlson, Lisa-Jo Baker, Maryanne Frawley, Saul Robles, and Melissa Reagan for their amazing work and support.

Greg Jackson, your design talents and ability to make vision into reality have been incredible throughout this journey. Thank you so much for all of your efforts.

The women of (in)courage—you are my extended network of sisters. If I listed all the ways each of you have blessed me, I would need to write another book! Thank you for your love, your grace, and the way you make me brave enough to go out there into the world with my words.

To my real-life girlfriends, thank you for all of the hours you spent talking with me about these things over coffee—for being my sounding board and safe place. You are a gift to me, and I thank God for you so often.

To my *Heart to Heart with Holley* readers, thank you for sharing this journey with me. This book started with you, and you helped me grow this seed of an idea into what it is today. Your beautiful fingerprints are all over the place here.

Most of all, thank you to Jesus for being willing to use me just as I am. I'm yours forever.

Notes

Chapter 1 A Heart-to-Heart Talk

1. Angie Smith, "Past and Pitcher," *Bring the Rain* (blog), May 24, 2008, http://angie smithonline.com/2008/05/the-past-and-the-pitcher.

Chapter 2 Who Am I, *Really*?

1. Marcus Buckingham and Donald O. Clifton, PhD, *Now, Discover Your Strengths* (New York: The Free Press, 2001), 51.

2. Ibid., 51–52.

3. Janet Kornblum, "Study: 25% of Americans have no one to confide in," *USA Today*, June 22, 2006, http://www.usatoday.com/news/nation/2006-06-22-friendship_x.htm.

4. Lisa-Jo Baker, e-mail message to author, March 17, 2010, used by permission.

Chapter 4 Why Do I Feel This Way?

1. Jennifer Warner, "No Joke: Laughter Is Universal," WebMD Health News, January 25, 2010, http://www.webmd.com/balance/news/20100125/ no-joke-laughter-is-universal?src=RSS_PUBLIC.

2. Peggy, February 12, 2010, comment on Holley Gerth, "The Rest of Your Story 28: How Do You Feel?" *Heart to Heart with Holley* (blog), February 11, 2010, http:// www.holleygerth.com/heart-to-heart-with-holley/2010/2/11/the-rest-of-your-story-28-how-do-you-feel.html#comment13223794.

Chapter 5 Where Am I Going?

1. Karen R., September 1, 2010, comment on Holley Gerth, "Two Little Words That Will Change Your World," *Heart to Heart with Holley* (blog), August 29, 2010, http:// www.holleygerth.com/heart-to-heart-with-holley/2010/8/29/two-little-words-that-will-change-your-world.html.

Chapter 6 Who's with Me?

1. C. S. Lewis, *The Inspirational Writings of C. S. Lewis* (New York: Inspirational Press, 1994), 278–79.

Chapter 8 What Does God Want Me to Do with My Life?

1. Marion, November 4, 2010, comment on Holley Gerth, "When You Want Life to the Full," *Heart to Heart with Holley* (blog), November 3, 2010 http://www.holleygerth. com/heart-to-heart-with-holley/2010/11/3/when-you-want-life-to-the-full.html.

2. Jennifer Stout, November 4, 2010, comment on Holley Gerth, "When You Want Life to the Full."

3. Bernice, November 7, 2010, comment on Holley Gerth, "When You Want Life to the Full."

4. Adrian Rogers, "Love Worth Finding," Adrian Rogers' Daily Devotional, March 23, 2010, http://www.crosswalk.com/devotionals/loveworthfinding/11627838/.

5. Bonnie Gray, "God's Love Is Perfected in De-Perfection," *Faith Barista* (blog), September 24, 2009, http://www.faithbarista.com/2009/09/gods-love-is-perfected-in-de-perfection.

Chapter 9 What Are My Next Steps?

1. Wayne Cordeiro, *Leading on Empty: Refilling Your Tank and Renewing Your Passion* (Minneapolis: Bethany House, 2010), 78–79.

2. Deidra Riggs, "Baby Steps (For Us Big Picture People at the Start of a Brand New Year)," (in)courage (blog), January 6, 2001, http://www.incourage.me/2011/01/baby-steps-for-us-big-picture-people-at-the-start-of-a-brand-new-year.html.

Chapter 11 What God Really Wants Your Heart to Remember

1. Ann Voskamp, *One Thousand Gifts: A Dare to Live Fully Right Where You Are* (Grand Rapids: Zondervan, 2011), 68.

2. Judy J., January 29, 2010, comment on Holley Gerth, "The Rest of Your Story 14: What Would You Edit?" *Heart to Heart with Holley* (blog), January 27, 2010, http://www.holleygerth.com/heart-to-heart-with-holley/2010/1/27/the-rest-of-your-story-14-what-would-you-edit.html.

3. Priscilla Shirer, *One in a Million: Journey to Your Promised Land* (Nashville: B&H Publishing Group, 2010), 172.

Go Deeper Guide

1. C. S. Lewis, *The Inspirational Writings of C. S. Lewis* (New York: Inspirational Press, 1994), 278–79.

About Holley

Holley Gerth is an award-winning writer, counselor, and life coach who loves sharing God's heart with women through words. She's done so through several books, bestselling products with DaySpring, and her popular blog *Heart to Heart with Holley*. Holley is also a cofounder of (in)courage, a web site for women that received almost a million page views in its first six months.

Holley shares her heart and home with her husband, Mark. She lives in the South, likes to say "y'all," and would love to have coffee with you so she could hear all about you too. Until then, she hopes you'll hang out with her online at www.holleygerth.com.

Hello, friend!

Thanks again for sharing this journey with me. I truly wish I could have a cup of coffee with you today and hear your heart. Until then, I hope we can stay connected in some other ways!

I'd love for you to stop by my place online, **www.holleygerth.com**. When you subscribe by email, you'll get free encouraging messages from me sent right to your inbox. I'm also on Facebook as Heart to Heart with Holley and Twitter as @HolleyGerth.

I'm thrilled that the Bloom (in)courage book club featured *You're Already Amazing* for spring 2012. So if you'd like to join some girlfriends in exploring this book, you can go to **www.incourage.me** and then to the book club section.

You can also find cards and gifts I created with DaySpring at **www.dayspring.com** and your local Christian store. I hope you'll discover some encouraging ways to share this message with the women in your life as well.

(Psst—I feel a little shy telling you all of this. But that's what friends do, right? Big gulp. Little smile. Thank you for letting me share with you!)

With Jesus you really are amazing, my friend. Keep believing that's true and living like you do!

Love,

Holley Gerth

PS: Together we can help women all over the world know they're amazing. A portion of author proceeds from this book will go to the Compassion International Leadership Development Program. To find out more about the program, visit **www.compassion.com**.

More exciting ways to enjoy *You're Already Amazing!*

Discover the dreams God has given you—
and then dare to pursue them.

Holley Gerth takes you by the heart and says, "Yes! You can do this!"
She guides you with insightful questions, action plans to take
the next steps, and most of all, the loving hand of a friend.

If your life isn't perfect . . .
If you've ever been disappointed . . .
If you feel stressed or tired . . .
This is for you.

"Holley Gerth is a fresh voice for every woman—
she echoes the voice of our Father."

—Ann Voskamp, *New York Times* bestselling
author of *One Thousand Gifts*

How would your life be different if you truly believed you're loved just as you are?

When we know we're truly loved, the response is to love in return—and that changes everything.

....

"I often say it doesn't have to be perfect to be beautiful. Holley Gerth shows women that's just as true for our hearts as it is for every other area of our lives."

—Myquillyn Smith, The Nester, author of *The Nesting Place*